The Language of
Mathematics

Mathematics Education Library
VOLUME 46

The titles published in this series are listed at the end of this volume.

Bill Barton

The Language of Mathematics

Telling Mathematical Tales

 Springer

Bill Barton
University of Auckland
Auckland
New Zealand
b.barton@auckland.ac.nz

Series Editor:
Alan Bishop
Monash University
Melbourne 3800
Australia
Alan.Bishop@Education.monash.edu.au

Library of Congress Control Number: 2007936207

ISBN -13: 978-0-387-72858-2   e-ISBN-13: 978-0-387-72859-9

Printed on acid-free paper.

9 8 7 6 5 4 3 2 1

springer.com

Dedication

This book is dedicated to my wife, Pip.

Acknowledgements

I wish first to acknowledge the academic inspiration and guidance I received from Ubiratan D'Ambrosio, Alan Bishop, Maria do Carmo Domite, and Andy Begg. Many of the ideas in this book emerged from their writing or in discussion with one or other of them. I am indebted to them for their mentoring and/or insights. There are many others who have contributed to my thinking about language and mathematics: my colleagues and students, reviewers of papers, and the many respondents at seminars or conference presentations. Thank you for your critical questions, original ideas, and helpful suggestions.

Special thanks also go to my language advisers, in particular: Shehenaz Adam (Dhivehi); Willy Alangui (Kankana-ey); and Tony Trinick (Maori).

John Mason helped me considerably with investigations into Double-Angle Geometry. He spent many hours exploring and analysing this environment, trying to answer my questions, and providing insights.

Three institutions have supported this work. My home university, The University of Auckland, has been generous in its leave and funding entitlements. The Department of Mathematics at The University of British Columbia, and the Departamento Didáctica de la Matemática of Universidad de Granada also hosted me for extended writing periods.

Others helped in the writing process. Thanks to the many who read and commented on my writing: in particular Ivan Reilly, Marcelo Borba, Trish Gribben, John Gribben, Emily Perkins, Karl Maughan, and Dave Ritchie.

And my love and appreciation to my wife, Pip, for being a colleague and co-researcher, discussant and questioner of new ideas, a writer's guide and proof-reader, a supporter and encourager, and a helper when the task was too big.

Contents

PRELUDE: MAORI MATHEMATICS VOCABULARY

Abstract: The Maori language was adapted for mathematical discourse during the 1980s. Several issues arose from this intensive time of specific language development. The story of this development, with examples of difficulties is outlined.

Keywords: bilingual mathematics, Maori language, mathematical discourse

1987. New Zealand. A warm, stuffy room in an old school building. A group of mathematics teachers have been working for a week discussing mathematics education for the indigenous Maori people. They have been developing mathematical vocabulary in the Maori language, and this evening they are working on statistical terms. They are trying to explain the difference between continuous and discrete data to a Maori elder. Examples are given: heights and shoe sizes; temperatures and football scores; time and money. The concept is grasped easily enough, but the elder must put forward suggestions for Maori vocabulary for use in mathematics classes. He will not transliterate to produce Maori sounding versions of the English words: for example, he might have tried *konitinu* for continuous or *tihikiriti* for discrete. He does try existing words for some of the examples that are given: *ikeike (height)*, and *tae (score)*— but these terms are not representative enough for the mathematicians in the room, and are rejected. Then he begins to try metaphors. At each attempt a short discussion amongst those mathematics teachers who know the Maori language quickly reaches consensus that the metaphor suggested will not do. Then he suggests *rere* and *arawhata*. Those of us in the room with only a little Maori understand the common meanings of these words as 'flying' and 'ladder'. It does not seem good enough for us. But the eyes of the good Maori speakers light up. They know that these words as a pair refer to the way a stream flows, either smoothly without a break, or in a series of little waterfalls over rocks. This mirrors the way that continuous data is information taken from a smooth stream of possible measurements, and discrete data is information that can only have particular values. Yes. New technical vocabulary is born.

Although I became aware of the importance of language in mathematics education while working in Swaziland in the late 1970s, my first serious involvement in this area was as part of this group of teachers developing vocabulary and grammar so that mathematics could be taught in the Maori language to the end of secondary education.

Maori is a Polynesian language brought to New Zealand by the first settlers over 1000 years ago. It was an oral language, and was not written down until European traders and missionaries came to New Zealand around 1800. As happened in other places in the world, significant European settlement signalled the start of a decline in the use of the indigenous language through familiar colonial processes. However, in the 1970s, a Maori cultural renaissance began. As part of this, bilingual primary schools were established, although mathematics and science were still mainly taught in English (Nathan, Trinick, Tobin, & Barton, 1993). Bilingual secondary schools developed during the 1980s, but Maori children remained alienated from mathematics and science. One response was the call for mathematics and science instruction in Maori (Fairhall, 1993; Ohia, 1993), and a small group was gathered together by the Department of Education to develop Maori mathematical language for this purpose (Barton, Fairhall & Trinick, 1995a). The group included teachers, mathematicians, mathematics educators, linguists, Maori elders, and Maori language experts. It worked under strict guidelines laid down by the Maori Language Commission, (these guidelines included a ban on the use of transliterations), and an imperative to ensure that any new language retained Maori grammatical structures.

This was a very exciting time for those involved. It felt as though we were in a crucible of language development, and we were all challenged both linguistically and mathematically. Linguistically the challenge was to produce vocabulary and grammar that had new uses (as far as Maori was concerned) but that was recognisably Maori in its structure, denotations, and connotations. There was a lot of use of metaphor, for example using *kauwhata* for a graphical framework or set of axes. *Kauwhata* refers to a rectilinear frame used for drying fish. Another vocabulary creation technique was to use standard Maori grammatical constructions, for example using standard suffixes for nominalising verbs, thus *pa* (to be related to, or concerning) is transformed to a noun, *panga*, with the meaning function. There was also an opportunity to resurrect old Maori words that had gone out of use with new (but related) technical meanings. The word *wariu* for 'value' had been used for many years, but was rejected as a transliteration. It was replaced by an old word, *uara*, that had fallen out of use, but meant the value or standing of someone.

Mathematically, those of us with expertise in the subject were challenged to accurately explain the meanings and functions of many mathematical terms and concepts. This proved more difficult than might be expected, particularly for the very basic concepts. For example, words like 'number' and 'graph' have meanings that shift in different contexts and at different stages of development of mathematical understanding. We were prompted to construct a genealogy of mathematical terminology that showed which words were base words in mathematical discourse and how other words could or should be derived from them. For example, 'multiple' is a child of 'number' and 'multiply'. This genealogical tree was not always obvious, nor is it unique.

The whole process was characterised by a cycle of collecting the terms being used in existing bilingual and immersion classrooms, taking the words and phrases back to Maori communities for their comment, writing up the results, and presenting this material to the Maori Language Commission for their decisions and ratification. The cycle was repeated three times over fifteen years, and the process and the resulting vocabulary and grammar have been published in a series of papers and dictionaries (Barton, Fairhall & Trinick, 1995a, 1995b, 1998; NZ Ministry of Education, 1991, 1994, 1995). It happened that the 'flowing' and 'waterfall' metaphors described above as words for 'discrete' and 'continuous' were eventually rejected in this process and replaced by words based on the Maori word *motumotu*—which means divided into isolated parts as islands are upon the sea.

So, was the Maori language successfully adapted to the teaching of mathematics? The answer is yes, ... and no. There is evidence that those taught mathematics in Maori are doing well (Aspin, 1995). Some students have been taught mathematics in Maori up to Year 13 (the final year of secondary school), but difficulties continue to exist in finding suitably qualified teachers (that is, those who are fluent in both Maori and mathematics), especially at senior levels.

However, those of us involved in the Maori mathematics language development had become increasingly uncomfortable with some aspects of our work. Somehow the mathematical discourse that had developed did not feel completely right, but we were unable to put our finger on why. We came to talk about this as the "Trojan Horse" phenomenon: mathematics education seemed to be a vehicle that led to the subtle corruption of the ethos of the Maori language (Barton, Fairhall & Trinick, 1998).

An example of grammatical corruption had happened during the vocabulary development process. It had been difficult to translate the concepts of positive and negative numbers. At the first meeting with the Maori Language Commission a discussion had resulted in a very rare agreement on the part of the Commission to alter the grammar of the language and use the direction-indicating adverbs *ake* (up) and *iho* (down) as adjectives for the noun *tau* (number). *Ake* and *iho* should only modify verbs, as in *heke iho* (fall down). But the adjectival uses *tau ake* (literally 'upwards number' for positive number) and *tau iho* (literally 'downwards number' for negative number) were to be permitted. Four years later, at the second meeting with the Commission, one member demanded that this decision be rescinded. She had heard some children in a school playground extend this grammatical misuse to their everyday discourse. A child had been heard to say "*korero ake*" (literally 'upwards talk') to refer to praise. *Ake* should not be used in this way as an adjective in correct Maori language. Under her angry imperative, an alternative formulation for positive and negative numbers was immediately found.

Our feeling that we had more fundamentally permanently changed the nature of the language was finally confirmed several years later. The example that epitomised the problem was that of the grammatical role of numbers. Classroom discourse that had developed during the 1980s used numbers grammatically very much as they are used in English. However, in Maori as it was spoken before European contact, numbers were verbal in their grammatical role (Trinick, 1999; Harlow, 2001; Waite, 1990).

What does "numbers were verbal in their grammatical role" mean? We are not familiar with numbers as verbs. A number does not seem to be an action. However it can be. In English there are verbal forms for the numbers 1 to 4: I can *single* someone out. I can *double* my bet. I can *triple* my earnings—well actually I can't, but someone else might be able to. A new school may even *quadruple* its enrolment over a few years. However, these forms are not the basis of our understanding of number. In everyday talk, numbers are usually used like adjectives. There are three bottles on the table. I have five fingers. Just as there might be green bottles on the table, and I have long fingers. (Technically, however, numbers are not adjectives. They are generally considered to have their own grammatical form).

In Maori, prior to European contact, numbers in everyday talk were like actions. The grammatical construction used would have been like saying that "the bottles are three-ing on the table", or that "my fingers five". Just as the bottles are standing on the table, or my fingers wiggle.

Our awareness of this old Maori grammar of number suddenly sharpened when we tried to negate sentences that used numbers. The construction that 'sounded right' was not the same as the construction that should logically follow from the classroom mathematics discourse.

Let us look at this in detail. To negate a verb in Maori the word *kaore* is used:

We are going to the house.	=	*E haere tatou ki te whare.*
We are not going to the house, we are returning.	=	*Kaore tatou e haere kit e whare, e hoki mai ke.*

Unlike English, where negating both verbs and adjectives requires the word 'not', in Maori to negate an adjective a different word is used, *ehara*:

This is a big house.	=	*He whare nui tenei.*
This is not a big house, it is a small house.	=	*Ehara tenei I te whare nui, he whare iti ke.*

In Maori, negating number uses the verbal form, *kaore*:

There are four hills.	=	*E wha nga puke.*
There are not four hills, there are three.	=	*Kaore e wha nga puke, e toru ke.*

Here was evidence that the classroom discourse that had been developed was against the original ethos of the Maori language. Numbers had been changed to become adjectival. While constructing the dictionaries and glossaries of mathematics vocabulary, the verbal nature of numbers was ignored, and a classroom discourse that treated numbers as they are in English was perpetuated. Thus the mathematics vocabulary process contributed to changes in Maori language use.

This experience led me to contemplate whether this had happened in other languages. I was interested in this example of the colonisation process, and I was concerned about the consequences for bilingual or multilingual mathematics education. But also, as a mathematician, I was curious about the mathematical concepts inherent in the original Maori usage of number. Would mathematics have developed differently if it had developed through languages in which numbers were verbal? More generally, I became curious about the way that mathematical ideas are presented differently in other languages.

So began a search for other examples, and an investigation into the mathematical consequences and the implications for mathematics education. I soon discovered that this material was not 'lost'. Many other people—linguists, anthropologists, mathematics educators, ethnomathematicians—had recorded and discussed unexpected ways of expressing mathematical thinking in many different languages. However these examples had not previously been considered from a mathematical point of view, and only briefly had educational consequences been considered (E.g. Pinxten, van Dooren, & Harvey, 1983, Chpt. 5). I quickly came to believe that there were important mathematical ideas to be found, and I began to change some of my views about mathematics itself. In addition, some of my thinking about mathematics education was being turned around. This book is the result.

INTRODUCTION

Abstract: An outline of the structure of the book is presented, making the argument that the language we use for everyday mathematical ideas presents us with valuable evidence and insights into the nature of mathematics.

Keywords: mathematical discourse, nature of mathematics

I begin the book by looking at the way people speaking different languages talk about mathematical ideas in their everyday conversation. I end up questioning some common beliefs about mathematics, its history, and its pedagogy.

The way we (English speakers) use numbers, the way we give directions, the way we express relationships, are all so commonplace that it is hard to imagine any other way of expressing these ideas. We take for granted the structures of the following sentences:

> There are four people in the room.
> The book costs forty-five dollars.
> Two and three are five.
> Turn left.
> Go straight on.
> The sun rises in the east.
> A dog is a mammal.
> He is not my father.
> I will either go shopping or read my book this afternoon.

But apparently simple English language statements turn out to be expressed quite differently in some other languages—so differently that it is often difficult to write in one language the equivalent of what is being said in another. Even when quantity is expressed in the simplest way—when we count—it is done in fundamentally different ways in different languages, as has been illustrated in the Preface. We are not talking about just different vocabulary. Nor is it a matter of differences in the underlying base of the number system, that is, whether it is a decimal system or one based on five or twenty. The variety occurs in the way languages express numbers, the grammar of mathematical discourse.

The first part of this book explores these differences. In order to further explore how other languages construct mathematical talk, I investigated languages as different as possible from my own first language of English. Distant languages are most likely to have unfamiliar structures. Unfamiliar structures are good clues in a search for different mathematical conceptions. Therefore most of the examples described are from indigenous languages rather than Indo-European languages: the Polynesian languages Maori, Hawaiian, and Tahitian; the Euskera language of the Basque people; Kankana-ey from the Cordillera region of The Philippines; Dhivehi from the Maldives; Kpelle from Liberia, and First Nation languages from North America.

The first part also includes some mathematical flights of fancy arising from the way various languages discuss numbers and shapes. The imaginings illustrate the possibility of different mathematical worlds. However the main point of this section is to lay down the evidence of language difference with respect to mathematical talk. I demonstrate the congruence between mathematics as we know it and the English language. Other languages are not so congruent.

Part II discusses what all this means for mathematics. Does it mean that mathematics as an academic discipline with very powerful practical applications is somehow different in different parts of the world? A bridge designed using mathematical theory surely stands (or falls) in the same way independently of the country it is built in, or of the language of the person who solved the equations of its design? Surely $1 + 1 = 2$ in Alaska, Nigeria, Tahiti, and Singapore? I argue for alternative answers to conventional questions about mathematics—where it comes from, how it develops, what it does, what it means. I challenge the idea that mathematics is the same for everyone, that it is an expression of universal human thought—and explain the questions about the bridge and $1 + 1$ posed incredulously above.

Another issue concerns the relationship between language and mathematical thought. Does the language we speak limit what we can say, do, and think mathematically? If this is so, we can infer serious consequences for mathematics if one language comes to dominate mathematical discourse, as English is doing within the international research arena. The question is wrongly posed. We probably do not need to focus on the limitations created by languages—languages are sufficiently creative as living structures to describe whatever we want to describe—but we should continue to explore the mathematical creativity embedded in other languages. New mathematical ideas (or old ideas given new roles) lie hidden in minority languages.

The third part of the book briefly discusses the consequences for the way we learn and teach mathematics. Can these linguistic insights into mathematics tell us anything about how we gain mathematical understanding? I make two fundamental suggestions. We should do more abstract activity, both in the early stages of learning mathematics, and when students are having difficulty. However, in saying this, the nature of useful abstract activity needs to be reconsidered. The second major suggestion is that undirected mathematical play is a good thing at all levels of education from early childhood to graduate level.

Does a better awareness of the links between mathematics and language lead us to practical strategies in mathematics classrooms? Educators have known for some time about the importance of talking, and the need for formal language development within the mathematics curriculum. And yet mathematics teachers do not universally use language activities. We re-examine the argument for these roles for language, and give some examples. In addition a plea is made for the importance of teaching about the nature of mathematics.

What about classrooms where more than one language is spoken, and what do the conclusions of Part I mean for students who learn mathematics in an unfamiliar language? Much writing on multilingual classrooms characterises such environments as full of problems. Without denying the complexity of the situation, the ideas in this book suggest that these classes have, rather, an abundance of resources. The question is how teachers can best utilise the linguistic potential therein.

Finally, having started with evidence collected from many languages of indigenous groups around the world, I end with a consideration of the particular issues faced by these groups with respect to mathematics education. A proper understanding of the link between language and mathematics may be the key to finally throwing off the shadow of imperialism and colonisation that continues to haunt education for indigenous groups in a modern world of international languages and global curricula.

For some time now, I have felt that many debates in mathematics education have been dominated by ideologies and theories, rather than comprehensively argued positions. These have sometimes reached ridiculous levels, such as the Math Wars in America where a professor went on a hunger strike, and people leapt into political action and lobbied with little regard for critical argument or evidence. I think that on a matter as important and deep-seated as this, there should be evidence of a more permanent kind that can clarify some of the debate. This book can be read as an attempt to interpret the evidence from language with respect to mathematics and mathematics education. The evidence presented here seems to me to support a weakly relativist philosophical position in that mathematics might have been created otherwise, and a social constructivist mathematics education position in that we develop mathematics in conjunction with our language. However readers would be mistaken to think that arguing these positions is what the book is about. The evidence is presented and interpreted.

Before we start, a short statement about what I mean by mathematics, and a few caveats. Mathematics is a tricky word, loaded, for the many non-mathematicians amongst us, with thoughts of school-teachers and textbooks and homework exercises. For mathematicians the meaning is richer, although there is considerable disagreement over its exact reference (Davis & Hersch, 1981). The problem for this book is that I wish to talk about mathematical things in general, and in contexts in which formal mathematics has no part. For example, as far as I am aware, in pre-European Maori culture, there was no area of knowledge or discourse equivalent to mathematics as understood today. How then can I talk about aspects of that culture being mathematical? The problem is circumvented in this book by mentally replacing the words 'mathematics' (or 'mathematical') with the phrase "(concerning) a system for dealing with quantitative, relational, or spatial aspects of human experience", or "QRS-system" for short. Thus any system that helps us deal with quantity or measurement, or the relationships between things or ideas, or space, shapes or patterns, can be regarded as mathematics. My translation allows the word 'mathematical' to be used much more widely than just to refer to things in mathematics texts or journals. If I want to talk about the smaller, formal, conventional world of academic mathematics as it is exemplified in schools and universities all over the world, then I will use the words "near-universal, conventional mathematics", or "NUC-mathematics" to refer to it. As an aside, I am told by sailing friends that NUC means "not under control" and refers to ships that have been abandoned at sea. Elements of this idea in NUC-mathematics will be illuminated in the following pages.

The caveats. Although I have taken the advice of many linguists, I do not claim to be a linguist myself. Nor do I claim fluency in any language other than English, despite a little Maori and a smattering of Spanish. I have used at least one first-language speaker of each language amongst my informants. Therefore the linguistic evidence is viewed from outside the discipline of linguistics, and from outside each of the languages used in the examples. This book, however, is about mathematics, so the languages are examined not so much for their linguistic characteristics, but for their mathematical ones.

A second caveat is that this work is written in English. To the extent that mathematical ideas differ between languages, the reflexive principle means that the ideas in this book would be different if they were written in another language. The discussion of other languages is from my point of view as an English speaker. If Euskera was my natural language, for example, then all the linguistic features quoted here would be seen in another way.

The third caveat is about coverage. I am mostly concerned about spoken language. Also there is no comprehensive coverage of all language families. Readers will note the lack of examples from Arabic and Asian languages, in particular Mandarin. Writing this book leaves me with a curiosity about those languages. I am certain that the written form is also important in mathematics, for example, it is significant that written Mandarin is iconographic while written English (and the other languages of my examples) is symbolic. Despite the importance of this issue, I will just acknowledge it and move on, leaving the fundamental influence of written language on mathematics for another time.

PART I

SPEAKING MATHEMATICS DIFFERENTLY

Chapter 1

SPACE: POINTS OF REFERENCE

Abstract: The way in which we talk about positions and locations is explored through
several languages. The different way of talking in the Tahitian language is extrapolated
into a geometrical system. The chapter concludes with a discussion of possible
social origins of geometry as it is usually taught.

Keywords: geometry, space, coordinate systems, Tahitian, Navajo

The quest to find new mathematical ideas in other languages took me first to Tahiti. The Maori and Tahitian languages are very close and Tahitian is still the first language of most Tahitians (unlike Maori). I was interested to find out whether the verbal grammatical role of number that we had found in Maori (see Preface) was the same in Tahitian.

In fact the verbal nature of numbers is well-preserved in Tahitian. In other words, the Tahitian language is linguistically more conservative, meaning that it has changed less under the influence of contact with other languages. It has been suggested that Tahitian has better retained its original syntax because King Pomare II had helped with the first translation (of the Bible), that is, a native speaker was involved. The first Maori translation, on the other hand, was a compilation of translations by various English missionaries. Foreign translators are likely to miss grammatical differences that are not part of their own linguistic landscape. An alternative explanation is that Tahitian language has undergone less change compared with Maori because the colonial policies of the French in Tahiti were more separatist than the assimilation policies of the English in New Zealand (Baude, 2003).

As an example of the difference between Maori and Tahitian, numbers are used with all the verbal particles in Tahitian. In both these languages, verbs are preceded by particles that indicate the tense or state of the action: *i* (indefinite past), *kua* (perfect or completed), *e* (imperfect or continuous, or indefinite), *ka* (inceptive or beginning), *a* (future), and *kia* (intentional). In Maori, *e*, *ka*, and *kia* are all used with numbers, although *e* is by far the most common. There is some argument about other particles despite recent grammars giving examples (Biggs, 1969; Harlow, 2001; Trinick, 1999, p. 106-11). In Tahitian, *e*, *ka*, *kia* and *kua* (in Tahitian the 'k' is replaced with a glottal stop) are all in standard usage (Académie Tahitienne, 1986).

But while investigating Tahitian another feature of Polynesian languages struck my mathematical imagination: the way in which location is described. There was a feature of the way one might talk about the position of something that was quite unusual to my English-language experience. A Tahitian speaker tends to use both himself (or herself) and the person being spoken to as reference points.

Before we explore this further, let us look at how location is described from a purely linguistic point of view, and then look at it from a mathematical point of view. Finally we will bring these two modes together, and explore the implications of this Tahitian language feature.

1.   WAYS OF LOCATING: LINGUISTIC FEATURES

So, how do we talk about location? The language we use depends on the situation. In English, in small scale situations such as describing people seated around a table, we tend to use phrases like "John is opposite Peter", or "John is a little way to the left", or "John is sitting two along from Peter". As the scale gets larger, for example when travelling by car, then we use the north, south, east, west compass points, "he lives ten kilometres north of the city". We also sometimes use another kind of reference, the position of something along a path, for example, "the house is on the road to the beach", or "the town is down-river from here". The use of these different methods of location in navigation is discussed later.

Focus on the directional aspect of location for a moment. Different languages, and different cultural groups, use the various methods in situations that are unlike English usage, and some languages have other systems that are not used in English. Australian Aboriginal people, for example, use the north/south/east/west system in very local situations, such as describing the position of people in a room, or where a picture might be placed on a wall (Harris, 1991). At very young ages, even before they can speak, Aboriginal children are aware of these directions whether they are inside or outside, in familiar surroundings or not.

Many Oceanic languages use a geographic direction-reference system (Senft, 1997). This is a response to the dominance of some particular geographic features. For example, if you live on an island, then *inland* and *seaward* have universal application in a way that they do not have in the interior of Mongolia. Rivers may provide another universally applicable reference, and, if you travel by foot, then *uphill* and *downhill* become significant when describing the location of destinations. For example, in the Solomon Islands language Longgu (Hill, 1997), there are two axes of orientation, one is East/West (derived from the rising and setting of the sun), and the other is inland and seawards (since most Longgu speakers are coastal dwellers). In this language, as in others, the geographical references are sometimes used on very small scales, such as describing the position of two stones relative to each other on the table. They can also be used in vertical locations, such as describing the position of lizards on a wall.

Knowing the direction of something is not usually sufficient to place its location; its distance is also needed. There are many different ways of expressing distance, for example the formalised measures (metres or inches), localised units (arms-length or a street block), using time, (a day's walk or five minutes' drive), or volume (a fuel-tank's distance).

The direction and distance of an object is still not enough to identify its position. We also need to say from where the direction and distance applies. For example, the reference point could be the speaker ("John is sitting on *my* left"), or it could be the person who is being spoken to ("John lives just round the corner from *you*"), or it could be another person or object known to both the speaker and the listener ("Granada is four hours drive south of *Madrid*"). Most languages use all three types of reference, although, as for directions, the area of application of the different forms are not always the same.

Polynesian languages, including Maori and Tahitian, have grammatical forms that make distinctions that are not present in English. In English we refer to *this* tree, to indicate that the tree is near to me, the speaker, or *that* tree, to indicate that the tree is at a distance from me, the speaker. In Maori and Tahitian, we can refer to this tree (*tenei rakau*), or that tree near to you, the listener (*tena rakau*), or that tree distant from us both (*tera rakau*). In general, reference is much less egocentric in Polynesian languages compared with English, and takes much more account of the point of view of the listener as well as the speaker. This occurs to the extent that acknowledgement of the social status of the listener relative to the speaker is also considered.

2.   WAYS OF LOCATING: MATHEMATICAL
SYSTEMS

Now let us leave language aside for a moment, and turn to mathematics. The position of an object in two dimensions (that is, on a surface) is generally defined using the Cartesian coordinate system, so named after Rene Descartes (1596 -1650), the French philosopher and mathematician who first used it in an algebraic way. (Coordinate systems of this kind were known earlier than this: Archimedes and Apollonius both used versions of this system in 200BC). From a single origin, two reference lines, or axes, are drawn at right angles. The position of a point is determined by two measurements: the first measurement is the distance along the horizontal line, and the second is the distance along the vertical one. The distance is positive if it is to the right or upwards, and negative if it is to the left or downwards (see Fig. 1-1).

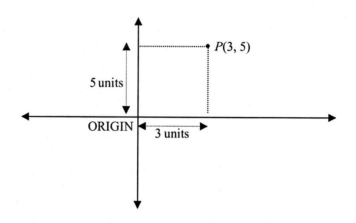

Figure 1-1. Cartesian Coordinate System

The second common way that position is determined, the Polar coordinate system, also uses a single origin, but only one reference line. The development of this system is usually attributed to Newton and Bernoulli, but some version of it is present in the work of Kepler.

The position of a point in this system is also determined by two measurements: one is the distance of the point from the origin, the other is the angle between the reference line and the line joining the point and the origin. The angle is positive if it is in an anticlockwise direction, and negative if it is clockwise. (In Fig. 1-2 the angles are measured in degrees, however mathematicians usually measure angles using radians).

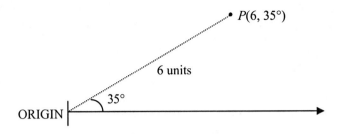

Figure 1-2. Polar Coordinate System

Another version of the Polar coordinate system is the bearings that are used in navigation and surveying. Here the vertical reference line represents north, and the angle measured in a clockwise direction is positive. Sometimes the compass points north, south, east and west (and intermediate ones such as nor-nor-east) are used (see Fig. 1-3).

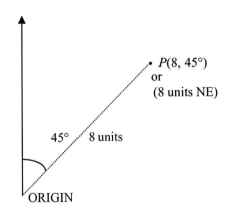

Figure 1-3. Bearings Coordinate System

3. LINKING THE LINGUISTIC AND MATHEMATICAL SYSTEMS

The Polar coordinate system corresponds to how we usually talk about position in English: we start from an origin, usually ourselves, and then describe how far away the object is, and its direction.

We also use, in common speech, a method of locating that is like the Cartesian coordinate system. This happens when we are describing the position on a grid—as in a city system of roads at right angles: "Go three blocks east and then two blocks north, the shop is on the corner". The reference directions may be more local, "go three blocks straight on, turn left and go a further two blocks", but the idea is the same. This might also occur when describing a book that is in a big bookshelf: "it is on the third shelf about half way along". We are also familiar with grid systems from finding streets on maps where numbers or letters are used to refer to particular squares in which the street is to be found. It could be argued that locating a passage in a book or newspaper is also Cartesian: "about half way down page 37" is a phrase incorporating two measurements of length.

The method of talking about the position of an object as a place on a path also has a mathematical correspondence in the idea of points on a curve, and is expressed as a function. This idea is discussed below in Part II, in the section on Metaphors.

We saw above that in everyday speech we conceive of each of the three necessary features of location (direction, distance, reference point) in more than one way, depending on what we are referring to, and on the language we are using. However, in standard school mathematics, there are only two representations: the Polar system or the Cartesian system. In the Polar system, direction is represented by a rotation from a reference line, distance is a standard linear measure, and the origin is a single point determined by the drawer of the graph. In the Cartesian system there are two linear distances at right angles, measured from one origin.

Are there other mathematical options? In everyday language, direction can be represented by local referents such us up, down, left, right, or by using several axes (east/west and inland/seaward). There are indeed mathematical equivalents of these alternative descriptions. For example, the development of the computer software LOGO, or Turtle Geometry, by Seymour Papert (1980) includes the four local commands (up, down, left, right) as possible movements of an object.

Formal mathematics also recognises the different ways of measuring distance. In advanced mathematics, distance is seen as an example of a 'metric' in the field of topology, and a metric can be defined in many different ways. There are mathematical applications in which a metric is defined using time, energy consumed, or the number of generations between species on the evolutionary ladder.

In order to explore further whether there are alternatives in mathematics that go beyond the way we describe measures or reference points, let us return to Tahitian and Maori, and the location systems implied by those languages.

The way that Tahitian and Maori can discusses location using both the speaker and the listener, is like using two origins, not one. This does have mathematical equivalents. Mathematically, if we have two origins, then the position of a point can be determined by two angles, one at each of the origins (see Fig. 1-4).

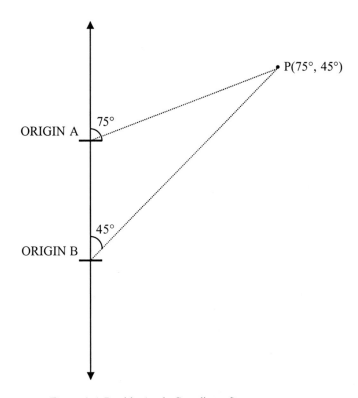

Figure 1-4. Double-Angle Coordinate System

Alternatively, still using two origins, the position of a point can be determined by the distance from each of the origins (see Fig. 1-5).

These systems are known within mathematics. In 1671 Newton, in his book *Method of Fluxions*, described ten different types of coordinate systems, including these ones. The systems described above have been used as practical methods in surveying for a long time. The word 'trigonometry' means 'measuring using a triangle' and is based on three points (such as two known reference points and the point of interest) making a triangle. Egyptians in the Nile valley and Babylonians in the Mesopotamian valley used triangles to survey land three or four thousand years ago. Modern global positioning technology uses the same idea. However, there is very little material about these systems as the basis of a mathematical approach to the study of space in general, and nothing in elementary texts. Why is this? Why are Cartesian and Polar coordinates preferred over coordinate systems using two angles and two origins?

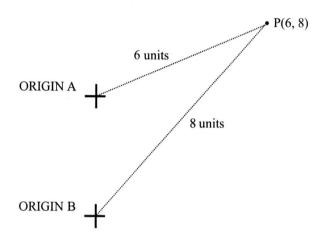

Figure 1-5. Double-Length Coordinate System

One answer to this question might be that such systems do not prove very useful—however, even if the surveying and positioning applications are not regarded as particularly useful, practicality is not the major criterion of merit in mathematics. Many mathematical studies throughout history have proceeded without useful applications in mind, but simply for the interest (and beauty) of the system itself, or as a result of questions posed by considering the mathematics alone. (Note, however, that virtually all mathematical developments were generated originally by some practical question, or through reflection upon aspects of real experience).

Another reason for focusing on single-origin systems might be that double-origin ones are not as mathematically rich. Perhaps this is true, however both double-origin systems generate beautiful curves with very simple equations (see Fig. 1-6). For example circles, which require second order terms (i.e. x^2) in the Cartesian system and trigonometric functions (i.e. sine) in the Polar system, are elementary first order equations in both double-origin systems. For example, in the Double-Angle system a circle is given by $\alpha = 2\beta$ where α and β refer to the angles from the two origins.

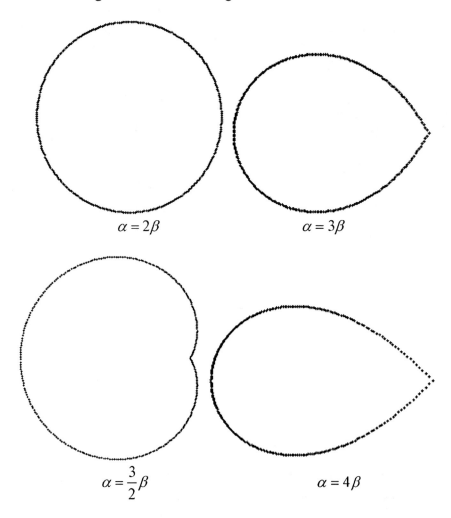

$\alpha = 2\beta$ $\alpha = 3\beta$

$\alpha = \dfrac{3}{2}\beta$ $\alpha = 4\beta$

Figure 1-6. Basic Curves of Double-Angle Geometry

When John Mason and I analysed these curves from a Cartesian perspective it turned out to be a trickier task than we had anticipated, and an interesting exercise in the careful use of trigonometric functions. In particular, it required analysing the intervals on which two trigonometric functions give the same positive value—which is more complicated than first imagined. We also discovered that letting α and β be angles greater than a full turn gave rise to beautiful "Sunset" diagrams (see Fig. 1-7).

If usefulness and mathematical richness do not fully explain the absence of double-origin systems in school mathematics, could part of the explanation be that those who developed mathematics had a predisposition to a single-origin point of view, a predisposition that was part of their language or culture? This hypothesis exemplifies the idea of this book: part of the reason that mathematics is like it is, is because its development has been influenced by the preferred ways of thinking and expressing thoughts of those involved. In particular, the languages of those who developed mathematical ideas helped to shape the mathematics that emerged. Mathematics could have taken many forms, the forms and preferences of NUC-mathematics (the near-universal, conventional mathematics of our schools) were not inevitable; they are the result of a particular historical trajectory that includes many social influences, including language.

Figure 1-7. Sunset Diagram

It is worth noting that the idea of a single origin can be found in other areas of intellectual thought that developed in the same linguistic and cultural milieu as mathematics. Descartes, according to Bertrand Russell (1946, p. 580), was the founder of modern philosophy as well as being responsible for the adoption of the Cartesian system in mathematics. The egocentric or subjective foundation of Descartes' philosophy, "*Cogito ergo sum*" ("*I think therefore I am*"), affected all philosophy derived from him. That is, philosophy followed a path in which everything, even one's own body, can be doubted, but not oneself. When I see something, according to Descartes, my own existence follows with certainty, but not the existence of the thing. Philosophy starts from one origin: oneself.

As in mathematics, there are alternatives to single-origin thinking in Philosophy. For example, Chinese philosophy includes the theory of Yin and Yang attributed to Fu Shi in the third or fourth millennium BC. Yin and Yang are the two opposing principles that embody the idea of universal change in their constant interaction. This has similarities with the logic of dialectics developed by Hegel (1770-1831), nearly two hundred years after Descartes. Both the theory of Yin and Yang, and dialectics, involve constant change, an issue that arises in the following chapter. More comments about the relation between mathematical and philosophical thought will be made then. In the meantime, it should be remembered that there is a logical error in Descartes' philosophy. As pointed out by Russell (1946, p. 589), this is linguistic in nature:

> "I think" is his ultimate premise. Here the word "I" is really illegitimate; he ought to state his ultimate premise in the form "there are thoughts." The word "I" is grammatically convenient, but does not describe the datum.

Another area of Western thought that has been affected by a single origin is that of anthropology. The anthropological concept of culture that dominated early work in the field, was one in which cultures were bounded, static, observable, fictional entities (Strauss, 2000, p. 88). One consequence was that early anthropological orientations were ethnocentric, defining other cultures in terms of (usually) Western culture. Thus other cultures were seen against a given background idea of culture—this is known as alterity (Corbey & Leerssen, 1991). This was one of the principal ways by which indigenous peoples "were objectified, dehumanized and designated as alterior" (McConaghy, 2000, p. 97). More relativistic, dynamic, and interactional models of culture now characterize the subject (Moore, 1997).

The suggestion that the fundamental ideas of mathematics, philosophy and anthropology are related to linguistic forms seems ambitious. Could just a small difference in predisposition when describing location in two different languages be relevant to a critique of the NUC-mathematical world? Let us suspend judgment a little.

After the exploration of location inspired by the forms of Polynesian languages, I was encouraged, and curious, to pursue other possible linguistic influences in NUC-mathematics. So continued the search for more evidence to justify the emerging hypotheses that mathematics has been affected by the language of its development, and that therefore mathematics could have developed in a way other than it did. In addition, it is possible that there is significant mathematical potential hidden in the way other languages represent mathematical ideas.

Chapter 2

SPACE: STATIC AND DYNAMIC WORLD VIEWS

Abstract: The way in which we talk about geometrical objects is explored through several languages. The different way of talking in the Navajo language is extrapolated into a geometrical system. Different ways of navigation are then analysed and the chapter concludes with a discussion of philosophical links with the development of mathematics.

Keywords: geometry, space, coordinate systems, Tahitian, Navajo, Pacific navigation, Zeno's paradoxes

The search for evidence of different ways of talking mathematically was hardly systematic. It was necessary to gather information about languages that had not been part of the development of NUC-mathematics. The information needed was how these languages express mathematical ideas. What discourse is used to talk about the quantitative, relational, or spatial aspects of peoples' experiences in their general, everyday language, both spoken and written?

The problem of how to access these languages was left largely to chance. After Maori and Tahitian, the languages Euskera, Dhivehi, and Kankana-ey were chosen because I happened to have contact with speakers of these languages who were also mathematicians. Some other languages, including African and First Nation American ones, provided examples in existing literature.

There were two relevant books that contained information of the type I was looking for. In the 1960s Gay and Cole (1967) had written about the Kpelle people of Liberia, in particular describing their language of logic and the effect it had on their understanding of logical relations. In the 1980s Pinxten, van Dooren, Harvey, and Soberon (Pinxten, van Dooren, & Soberon, 1987) had built on an earlier anthropological study (Pinxten, van Dooren, & Harvey, 1983), and written about the geometrical language of the Navajo. This latter work tied in with the verbal numbers of Polynesian languages since, in Navajo, what we know as geometrical objects (circles, squares, lines, spheres) are expressed verbally.

1.   WHAT ARE VERBAL SHAPES?

Verbal shapes? Let us think about this first in English. Shape is expressed in many ways. Consider the geometric idea of a square. In everyday language shapes are usually characteristics of something: a square piece of paper, a square table. But I can ask someone "to fold a piece of paper into a square", in the same way as I might ask them to fold it into a bird. The squareness is expressed like an object. Or I could ask them "to square the piece of paper" in the same way as I might ask them to screw it up. The squareness is expressed as an action.

Try another shape. We can say that a shape is a triangle (which makes the idea of a triangle into a thing), or that a shape is triangular (which makes this idea a characteristic of a thing), or that something is triangulating (which makes the idea into an action). Notice that the form of the word for the adjective and verb are clearly derived from the noun.

These three ways of speaking about a shape work for a square, a triangle, a circle (we could have a circular piece of paper, we could ask people to sit in a circle, the birds might circle the treetops), and for a line (planes may fly in a linear formation, we are asked to stand in a line, people line up at a ticket office). But in mathematical discourse, and especially with more complicated mathematical shapes, a shape is usually described as an object or as a characteristic. We can draw a pentagon, and something may be pentagonal, but it sounds clumsy to ask someone to "pentagonalise a piece of paper". Notice that in all these examples, the adjectives are either the same as, or derived from, the noun: square—square, circle—circular, line—linear, pentagon—pentagonal. The noun form is privileged in English; it seems to be the base concept in everyday language and in mathematical discourse. The derivations of these words are given in dictionaries as from nouns. It is, of course, possible to use any form, and even to construct odd but understandable forms ("decagonal"), however noun forms are more common, and sound better.

In Navajo the opposite is the case:

A basic characteristic of the Navajo world view ... is the fundamentally dynamic or active nature of the world and everything in it. ... [This is a] basic perspectival difference from Western thought and language. (Pinxten, van Dooren, & Harvey, 1983, p. 15).

… a cosmos composed of processes and events, as opposed to a cosmos composed of things and facts. (Witherspoon, 1977, p. 49).

In the grammar of the language, this feature is expressed through verbs. This does not mean that the verbs can be considered as spatial terms themselves, rather the grammar of the language is such that a particular verb can only be used with a certain group of objects that have a particular spatial characteristic. So the geometrical reference is carried in the verb, rather than in the noun. For example, the idea of planeness (a flat expanse in two dimensions) is associated with the verb sikaad: tó sikaad = a layer of water spreading out; diih dikon tsin sikaad = a wooden floor spreading out (Pinxten, van Dooren, & Harvey, 1983, p. 93). It is not possible to use this verb to describe land, on the other hand, because land has a certain thickness, even though it does spread out.

The mathematician in me is intrigued by the idea of verbal expression of shapes. Could this make a difference mathematically? Does the way we think about the idea of triangularity affect what we understand about it? It was interesting to play the mind-game of what the study of shape might be like if it had developed verbally. How might geometry be different?

Let me be clear that this is my mind-game, not a Navajo mind-game. The way I am using the idea of "circle as an action" is my conception of that idea, not a Navajo one. For example, the idea of circular may be used to describe an object with a circular shape or outline. In Navajo this would be indicated by a verb, in English by an adjective. But I have taken the idea of circular as only an action: I am playing a mind-game where a circle is something you do, and I am using the verbal function of action from English, not from Navajo.

Imagine, then, that circularity is an action, not an object, thus we must talk about circling, not a circle. Working mathematically, it is necessary to make this idea more formal, that is, to explore the details of what makes the action exactly circular, and to distinguish it from actions that are not circular. I need to be able to define circling, to categorise different circlings, to describe the characteristics of circling, to know how circling is related to other shape-actions, and to understand how it changes.

2.   BIRDS AND ORBITS

If a circle is an action, then it is necessary to imagine movement and not a static picture. One way to do this is to make yourself into the actor. Think of yourself as a bird circling a tree. For the moment, let us say that you are flying at a constant speed. Now, what is it about the way that you are flying that means you are flying in a circle (circling) and not a square (squaring) or an ellipse (ellipsing)? It is the fact that you are turning at a constant rate all the time. To be squaring, for example, you would fly straight, and then turn suddenly at the corners. So the defining feature of circling is what is called constant angular velocity.

What would be different if you were turning more quickly (but still at a constant rate)? You would be circling more tightly. Assuming constant speed, differently sized circlings are characterised by different angular velocities (that is, the rate at which you are turning).

If, on the other hand, we kept the angular velocity constant, we could then change the size of our circling by changing our speed: a greater speed would result in wider circling, a slower speed would make it tighter.

> **Constant speed, constant rate of turn.**
> If the speed of both birds is the same,
> then the bird is turning more quickly in the smaller circling.
> If the rate of turn of both birds is the same,
> then the bird is flying more slowly in the smaller circling

Figure 2-1. Flying in smaller circles

That takes care of the size of the circling. What other characteristics of circling might we be interested in? Perhaps the length of time it takes to get back to where you started. Perhaps the way it is oriented to the ground; are you circling in a horizontal plane or is your circling tipping (like the fairground ride I know as an Octopus)? Or are you circling in a vertical plane like a Ferris Wheel?

In this geometry, how does circling relate to other shape-actions? Again let us imagine that we are a bird, flying at a constant speed and turning at a constant rate so that we are circling. Let us gradually change one of these variables: instead of turning at a constant rate, let us steadily increase the rate of turn, making us turn tighter and tighter. What does our path look like now? We would be spiralling inward. And if we steadily decreased the rate of turn as we are flying at constant speed, we would then be spiralling outward.

This means that circling is actually a special case of spiraling.

What happens if we are not turning at all, if the rate of turn is zero? Then, of course, we are flying along in a straight line (lining), thus lining is a special case of circling (rate of turn is also constant—but it is zero). Similarly, if we turn at an infinitely fast rate we will simply be staying at the same spot.

The same effect can be obtained from changing the speed, but keeping the rate of turn constant. If you fly at a faster constant speed, then the circle will be bigger—at infinite speeds you will fly in a straight line. If you fly at a slower constant speed, then the same rate of turn will make you fly in a smaller circle—and if you stop, of course, you will just turn on one point. So pointing (the action of being in one place) is a special case of circling.

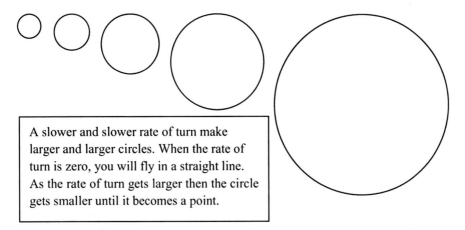

A slower and slower rate of turn make larger and larger circles. When the rate of turn is zero, you will fly in a straight line. As the rate of turn gets larger then the circle gets smaller until it becomes a point.

Figure 2-2. Flying in points and lines

In coordinate geometry, a circle is a special case of a family of curves known as conic sections that also include parabolas and ellipses. How would you fly in order to describe these shapes? Think about runners sprinting around a sports arena. This is not an ellipse, but it is similar, and will do while we think about what is happening to them. They are running at more or less constant speed, not turning at all as they go along the straights, and then leaning into the corners at each end. So the rate of turn is changing during the circuit: from zero, to turning, to zero again, to turning again. So it would be for an ellipse. In this shape there are no straights, so the rate of turn would never reduce to zero, but it would decrease, increase, decrease and increase again, all in a steady fashion.

Ellipsing can also be done by turning steadily, but changing your speed. Fly with a constant rate of turn, and then steadily increase your flying speed, then decrease it, then speed it up again, and decrease it again. The effect will be to elongate circling into ellipsing.

There is a situation that exemplifies ellipsing: that of planets orbiting around the sun. Think of yourself as the planet. What is happening? In fact it is a combination of the two situations we have been describing, since both the flying speed and the rate of turn are changing. As you approach the sun, the pull of gravity speeds you up and turns you towards that burning orb. But (fortunately) you are travelling too fast to become an Icarus, and you fly by. Now the sun is close and the pull of gravity is strongest, and you are forced to turn quite strongly in the direction of the sun. But your speed is such that you go right around the sun, and head back from whence you came. But now you are moving away from the sun, and again it starts to pull you back, slowing you down. But as you get well past it the pull gradually decreases. Nevertheless it is enough to slow you down, slower and slower, and to turn you around again. You are a long way away, turning slowly, and your speed is quite low. So low that that distant pull of the sun is enough to pull you back again for another approach. Uh-oh, here we go again.

The mathematics of this situation is well-known in conventional terms. But it is interesting to compare what is done in astronomy, and what might be done if the mathematician was on the planet (of course this is exactly the situation for artificial satellites that are thrown up into orbit around earth or the moon). What do astronomers do, when they think they have found a new heavenly body? They take observations of its position (with reference to the earth, sun, or centre of gravity of the solar system, and also using a reference plane). When they have enough observations over a great enough period of time, then they use these positions to fit an ellipse. If they have enough positions (theoretically three are enough to determine an ellipse, but in practice more are used to minimise the effect of measurement error), then the ellipse can be mapped accurately, and it is then checked against a data-base of ellipses of known heavenly bodies kept on a big computer in Harvard. New ellipse? Bingo. New heavenly body.

Now, in Action Geometry we have used speed and rate of turn as the basic elements, not position. If the mathematician was on the planet, then rather than determine position relative to some reference point as the basis for calculations, they might rather use the speed and rate of turn as the basis for predicting where they were going.

What about other shapes. Can a square be an action? There are all those sharp corners. It is here that we see more clearly the differences in the items of interest between Action Geometry and conventional (Static) Geometry. If you are travelling in a square, then you must either stop and turn, or turn infinitely quickly, at the corners. The way you trace the shape becomes a combination of flying speed and turning speed. Also, the time taken on each side is important (if a constant flying speed is assumed). Of course it is possible to describe any shape at all using either Action Geometry or Static Geometry. Notice, however, that shapes without sharp corners are more easily described in Action Geometry. Action geometry would privilege such smoothly curved shapes, but would have a difficult time describing the constructions of Euclidean geometry.

Seymour Pappert's computer environment LOGO (often known as Turtle Geometry) appears to be a mix of Static and Action geometry (Abelson & diSessa, 1980). In this environment the screen becomes a field on which the icon (originally represented as a turtle) can be made to move. The original version enabled the user to move forward or back a given length, or to turn a given angle. This uses the idea of movement as its base, but still characterises movement as going from one point to another. A true Action geometry environment would allow the user to adjust speed and rate of turn along a continuous path, not iterate a number of small positional movements to make a path.

3. EUROPEAN AND PACIFIC NAVIGATION

A parallel exists between the two geometries being described and two ways of conceptualising navigation. The different conceptual systems possible for navigation first came to my attention when I read about the navigation techniques of Pacific peoples (Gladwin, 1970;

Hutchins, 1983; Irwin, 1997; Kyselka, 1987; Lewis, 1975; Thomas, 1987; Turnbull, 1991). The basis of their navigation is to determine where they are on their journey, not their exact position.

Consider traditional navigation as it developed through European navigators. From the early art of "way-finding" (Collinder, 1954), a system evolved that required a number of sightings of the sun or stars, and measurements of time, so that position could be accurately located on a map. The history of this development, and the technological effort and expenditure that went into it, is described in Sobel's book Longitude (1995). One way of thinking about this is to imagine that a grid has been constructed upon the world and the position of places of interest are known with respect to this grid. Thus if you can locate your position on the grid, then you know your position in relation to the places you came from or are going to. This system is now developed to such an extent that using satellite GPS (Global Positioning Systems), a hand-held computer will give you a read-out of your position to within a metre. I have friends who, in thick fog, sailed out of a narrow gap between two rocky outcrops using only such equipment and their charts. If you use this system then your aim is to be constantly aware of your position, and of how far you are from known critical points.

Notice that this system relies on a reference system that has been created by humans. The original references were features of the real world (headlands, islands, reefs), but the latitude and longitude grid that has developed from these is artificial.

Now consider traditional Pacific navigation. The experienced navigators have the equivalent of charts in their minds, but these are not position charts, they are a set of features and signs that indicate the path that they will travel. This path is not always a straight line, rather it goes from landmark—or, rather, sea-mark—to sea-mark. For example they are likely to know more about the direction of their destination and how long it will take to get there, than how far away they are from it. In a well-documented experiment a navigator did two return journeys from Hawaii to Tahiti in a replica Polynesian double canoe, and travelled along the same dog-leg shaped path each time (Kyselka, 1987). Indeed, on one occasion, the following tracking ship with modern navigation aids, lost all power and had to reply on the canoe to reach its destination. Sea-paths do not, however, always cover the same ground: they depend on weather, seasons and sea conditions.

Such a means of travel is, of course, very common for people travelling by land. If I drive from my city to another three hours away, there is no need for a map. There are many signs to tell me that I am on the right path, and as I become familiar with the journey. I will note landmarks and sights along the way, and I will have my favourite stopping places, from where I will know how long it is until I reach my destination. At any point I may not even know in which direction my destination lies, but, nevertheless, I am confident that I am "on track". In this system it is important to know, first, that you are on the right path, and secondly, how long it will take to reach other critical places on the path.

The difference between what we can call Position Navigation and Path Navigation can be illustrated by two ways in which movement is characterised. In the televised animations that accompany America's Cup yacht race coverage, the speed of the yachts is visually represented by a trail of dots behind each boat. These dots are created for the animation from the highly accurate GPS equipment on board by recording the position at regular time intervals. If the dots are close together, that means that the boat is going slowly, if they are spreading out, then the boat is increasing speed, and so on. Speed represented by position.

Compare this with the idea of etak (Akimichi, 1985; Gladwin, 1970, Chpt. 5; Gunn, 1970), one of the conceptual formulations of travel of the Pacific navigators. When a canoe is moving along its path, then we can imagine that there is an island ahead that we need to pass by (let us say to the right of it). As we pass by, this island will appear to move from nearly directly in front, to ahead but on the left, to abeam on the left, to behind and to the side, to nearly directly behind. It is as if the island moves while the boat stays still. This idea is etak, and Pacific navigators use it to describe islands or features that cannot be seen (perhaps because they are over the horizon) as indicators of how well they are travelling down their path. Motion is thus represented by changing bearings of sea-marks.

What is the correspondence between Position Navigation and Path Navigation and Static and Action geometries? Position navigation focuses on reference points and distances, using them to find the bearing that must be travelled. Path navigation focuses on pathways and speed, using them to find the direction of the next sea-mark. The first has static references, the second has active ones.

The examples of planetary orbits and navigation illustrate different ways of conceptualising space. One way uses the basic idea of static position with reference to an origin. Another way has movement through the space as the base idea. Each way of seeing makes some things easy and other things complicated. In the study of space that is part of NUC-mathematics, objects and position are treated first, and movement (speed and turn) is a more complicated idea that is treated later. This section has tried to illustrate that it is possible to begin a study of space using movement, and then think about position at a later time.

Note that there is nothing that has been mentioned about Action geometry that cannot be described in terms of conventional Static geometry. The reverse is also true. We can do Static geometry in terms of Action geometry, or vice versa. (Note that describing the orthocentre of a triangle would be complicated in Action geometry and easy in Static geometry, and the opposite is true for describing a changing spiral). The point is that we do not do this, or, we tend not to, certainly not at first. This is because some things are easier, or more natural, than others, depending on which geometry you are using. This is not an unusual idea. In conventional geometry we have several systems, for example the Cartesian coordinates and Polar coordinates mentioned above, and we use the system that is easiest for what we are trying to do: the Cartesian systems for straight lines and some curves, the Polar system for circles and other curves. However it should not surprise us that the systems that are in common use are not all the systems available.

4.   LINKING THE LINGUISTIC
AND MATHEMATICAL SYSTEMS

We are predisposed to see space using particular basic ideas. It is suggested that part of the reason that NUC-mathematics is the way it is results from the linguistic and cultural orientation of those who developed it. Western thought is culturally and linguistically predisposed to reference and position, whereas, for example, the Navajo one is predisposed to action and movement. Let us again use the word privilege to describe what is happening: languages, as the expression of cultures, privilege different ways of thinking about shapes and space.

The investigation starting from the dynamic Navajo world view has given us something more substantial than the flight of imagination based on differences in the few words in Tahitian used to describe the position of an object. Now we are talking about a whole way of understanding shape and the potential geometrical world that that creates: a world with different base concepts, with different foci of attention, with different relations and contexts, with different applications.

At the end of the previous chapter, we noted that the Chinese philosophy of Yin and Yang, and the logic of dialectics, each provided philosophies with more than one origin in contrast to Descartes egocentric theories. It was suggested that there might be parallels with graphical representation being developed through a single-origin model based on Descartes ideas, with double-origin models being relatively ignored in Western mathematics.

The parallel can be extended to the idea of Static and Dynamic geometries. The idea of constant change is at the heart both of the theory of Yin and Yang, and of dialectics. Western philosophy, on the other hand, developed through the Greeks. Rotman (1987, p. 62) writes:

> [The Greeks were] logically persuaded that change and plurality, however much they seem real to us, must be illusions. … Parmenides, and more famously his disciple Zeno, gave many arguments defending his unitary static cosmos. Those that survive are principally in the form of paradoxes which forced their interlocutors into accepting that the ideas of motion and plurality were inherently contradictory and incoherent, and were therefore, by a reductio ad absurdum argument, not real.
>
> Zeno's celebrated paradoxes … had a profound affect on the structure of Greek thought—on its mathematics no less than its theology and cosmology. …
>
> … In terms of definition, [the Greeks] denied any role to motion. All their objects of Greek mathematical thought such as numbers, ratios, points, figures, and so on, were characterized as wholly static fixed entities so that, for example, the figure of a circle was defined as the locus of points equidistant from some given point and not as the path of a moving point.
>
> … The Zeno-Parmenides interdiction of motion … engendered within Greek mathematics … an attachment to visually concrete icons which influenced mathematics from the time of Euclid to the Renaissance (and beyond: a version of Parmenidean stasis is central to the dominant present-day conception of mathematics in which mathematicians are supposed to apprehend eternal truths about entities –'structures' – in an unchanging, timeless, static, extra-human world).

Of course Parmenides' and Zeno's paradoxes can be rewritten to make the opposite conclusion. Consider the paradox of the arrow:

> If everything when it occupies an equal space is at rest, and if that which is in locomotion is always occupying such a space at any moment, the flying arrow is therefore motionless. (Aristotle *Physics* VI:9, 239b5).

That is, time is made up of indivisible moments, in each of which the arrow occupies a space that is just the size of itself. Hence it is motionless. But let us pretend that we are in a world based on motion, then the argument might go like this:

> Arrows move from bow to target, and in any time interval, no matter how small, they traverse a length. Since they are always traversing, arrows never occupy any position.

The conclusion of the paradox is that the arrow never occupies space.

What is interesting is that the resolution of the paradox (in modern terms, the way we define instantaneous velocity), is to calculate the speed over a small distance, and to define as instantaneous what happens as these distances get smaller and smaller—although they never actually become a single point. This resolution never gives up the idea of point: position is the basic tool we have to define our world. The paradox could, however, be resolved by defining position as the path traversed by the head of the arrow as the time interval gets shorter and shorter, without ever requiring time to be reduced to an instant. This is equally as satisfactory (or unsatisfactory) as the conventional resolution.

The other area of Western thought identified as being initially dominated by a single origin perspective was that of anthropology. As with philosophy, the modern concepts of culture are dynamic and take account of cultural development. For example, Welsch's (1999, p. 202) transculturalism in which:

> The basic task is not to be conceived as an understanding of foreign cultures, but as an interaction with foreignness. Understanding may be helpful, but is never sufficient alone, it has to enhance progress in interaction.

The questioning of egocentricity and stasis in Western thought is taking place in philosophy and anthropology. This book is doing it in mathematics.

In Part II of this book we look more closely at how mathematical worlds might be created by language, and the consequences of this. But before that we turn to other aspects of mathematical systems. Are the examples of different ways of talking about quantity and relationships, similar to those we have described about space? Numbers, it turns out in the next chapter, might seem like the simplest idea, but in fact they have caused an awful lot of trouble. And, in Chapter 4, we look at examples from other languages of people making sense of relationships of various kinds. How are categorisations made, how do we explain human relationships, and how do we create logical arguments using these relationships?

Chapter 3

QUANTITY: TRAPPING NUMBERS
IN GRAMMATICAL NETS

Abstract: The grammar of numbers is explored through consideration of Maori, Kankana-ey, and Maldivian languages. This is used to discuss the ways in which we refer to numbers in English, and how that hides important mathematical ideas. The mathematical benefits or drawbacks of different languages are considered.

Keywords: Maori, Kankana-ey, Dhivehi, grammar of numbers

Chapters 1 and 2 have dealt with the way two spatial topics are described in different languages: defining position and finding your way. In this chapter we return to the topic of quantity in QRS-systems. (Remember that this is my code for a system for dealing with the quantitative, relational or spatial aspects of human life). Quantity involves number and measurement. The relationship between them is discussed later in Chapter 6. Initially, I want to look at numbers only, focussing on their grammar. The different bases of number systems have long been investigated and are not reviewed here (see, for example, Menninger, 1969; Lean, 1995).

My quest for other ways of talking about numbers began, it will be remembered, by the realisation that the Maori (and Tahitian) languages treated numbers in a way that was unusual for an English speaker. Before we examine this in detail, let us first think about the grammatical roles played by numbers in English, both in general discourse, and also when discussing mathematics.

Numbers are regarded, in English, to have their own grammatical category. However, in general, everyday discourse, they act more like adjectives than anything else: they seem to describe a characteristic. I could ask you to give me three pens, just as I might ask you to give me green pens. Threeness is a characteristic of the group of pens you are giving me, as is the fact that they are green.

In mathematical talk, numbers shift their grammatical nature. We discuss numbers as objects in themselves. We can say that five is a prime number, in the same way that we might say that a whale is a sea-going mammal. Numbers themselves have characteristics, for example primeness, or evenness, or divisibility. A number is often, grammatically, used as a noun.

Sometimes numbers are used in their adjectival sense and in their nominal sense in the same sentence. "Three fives are fifteen." The three is adjectival, the five and fifteen are nominal—the five is even made into a plural (there are three of them, just like you can have three hugs or three kisses). The important point is that all of this feels quite natural in English, we are not even aware of the different grammatical uses of number words, and we move between them quite easily depending on what we are trying to say.

This is not the case with all languages.

1.   EMERGING NUMBERS: POLYNESIAN LANGUAGES

During the development of a Maori mathematical vocabulary, it was realised that numbers in old Maori (before European contact) were verbal in their grammar. There are still traces of the verbal use in modern Maori. The way that they are usually used in modern Maori is becoming increasingly like the way they are used in English. There is debate about whether this constitutes corruption or is evidence of a modern, living language. More on that later, let us first briefly review the verbal evidence.

In modern Maori grammars, as in English, numbers are regarded as having their own grammatical category. However, for the reasons outlined in the Introduction (the way a number statement is negated) and at the beginning of Chapter 1 (the use of particles with number words), this category is verbal in nature compared with the more adjectival English use.

A recent Grammar of the Maori language (Harlow, 2001) describes the verbal nature of numbers in Maori, focusing on their use with verbal particles. *E, ka, kua* and *i* are all tense markers, and kia indicates a wish or a command. All are used with numbers. Two examples are below. I have added my more verbal translation:

There are two houses in this street

(Maori translation):	*E rua*	*nga whare*	*kei roto I tenei rori*
(My translation):	Two-ing are	the houses	in the street
(Given translation):	The houses that are in the street are two in number		

Give me five pens

(Maori translation):	*Homai*	*kia rima*	*nga pene*
(My translation):	Give me	let them be fiv-ing	the pens
(Given translation):	Give me, let the pens be five in number		

Notice how the Grammar writer has tried to maintain the English grammatical role for the number words, but in doing so has distorted the way the sentence is constructed in Maori. It is actually consistent to think of the numbers as pure verbs.

Second language Maori speakers usually use the particle *e* in front of numbers, but often otherwise treat numbers as they are treated in English. In the mathematics classroom this is particularly true. When this happens the *e* makes no sense except that "it sounds right".

In order to make a number into a noun, it must be preceded by an article: *te* (the singular), *nga* (the plural), or *he* (a). So, to translate a mathematical sentence:

Five is a prime number

(Maori translation):	*He tau toitu*	*te rima*
(My translation):	A prime number (is)	the five

Thus, for Maori, having a mathematical discourse involves changing the grammar. In English the adjectival and the nominal use of 'three' do not involve a change to the word or its accompanying words—it is only a matter of word order. In Maori the change involves changing verbal particles (for example, *kia*) to an article (for example, *te*). This makes it sound strange to a native speaker.

2. NUMBERS TRAPPED AS ADJECTIVES: KANKANA-EY

The situation is more difficult for some other languages, where a conventional school-level mathematical discourse forces even greater alterations of accepted grammar. We will now look at the language Kankana-ey, spoken around Sagada in the mountainous regions of the northern Philippines.

Kankana-ey is a language that uses an unusual feature when putting an adjective with a noun. In linguistics this is called a ligature. This is a small word, in this case *ay*, that is put between an adjective and a noun. Thus you would say (the adjective comes first in Kankana-ey as in English):

tall children	=	*anandu ay ungung-a*
wide rice terrace	=	*nalawa ay payew*
white stone	=	*puraw ay bato*

This construction is also used with numbers:

four children	=	*epat ay ungung-a*

Compare the two sentences:

Do you have a raw banana?	=	*Ay wada nan maata ay baat?*
Do you have five bananas?	=	*Ay wada nan lima ay baat*

Thus, as far as the language is concerned, a number is grammatically fixed as a characteristic of something, like its colour or its dimensions. In fact the descriptive role of numbers is even stronger than that of some other adjectives. For example, when it is the existence of the characteristic that is being emphasised, then the structure changes for all characteristics except numbers, which is the only one that keeps the ligature:

The children are tall.	=	*Anandu nan ungung-a.*
The stone is white.	=	*Nan bato et puraw.*
There are four children.	=	*Wada nan epat ay ungung-a.*

It is possible, as in English, to construct sentences where the things being counted are suppressed but understood to be present. This grammatical feature is called ellipsis. For example the noun 'people' can be dropped in the sentence:

There are six people in the house, five are women	=	*Wada nan enem ay ipogaw sinan abong, babbai nan lima.*

Also it is possible to give just a number as an answer to a "How many?" question:

How many birds are in the tree? Five.	=	*Kaat nan kuyat nan wada id kaiw? Lima*

So far, the examples given are the same for English. Now consider:

Five pigs are too many.	=	*Adu unay nan lima ay boteg.*
	≈	Plenty too much are five pigs.
Five is too many	=	*Adu unay nan lima.*
	≈	Plenty too much are five.

Using numbers on their own can only happen when the object can be added to the sentence without change, as if it was always there in parentheses. Here is the difference: in English we can use numbers on their own by changing the grammar. Notice that in the example above the verb 'are' changes to 'is' when the noun is dropped. The effect of this is to make the number into a single object, as opposed to a characteristic.

The use of a ligature, *ay*, makes it more difficult than in English for the number word to act like a noun. It is trapped in its descriptive function. In schools in Sagada where Kankana-ey is used, there is noun-like usage of the number words in mathematical sentences:

Take away two from three.	=	*Kaanem nan dua isnan tulu.*
Remove the toy from the jar.	=	*Kaanem nan ay-ayam isnan gusi.*
Two is small compared to ten.	=	*Ban-ban-eg nan dua no nan simpoo.*
The stone is small compared to the tree.	=	*Ban-ban-eg nan bato no nan kaiw.*
Five is smaller than eight.	=	*Nan lima kitkittoy nu sin wao.*
Willy is shorter than Peter.	=	*Si Willy et ap-aptik nu si Peter.*

However this usage sounds very odd to a native speaker of Kankana-ey, whereas the structure sounds fine to an English-speaker. Kankana-ey is poorly suited to the mathematical use of number.

So numbers in Kankana-ey are trapped in their descriptive, adjectival function. Numbers in Polynesian languages are trapped in their active, verbal function. Although mathematical discourse, and the use of numbers as objects, is possible in both languages, strange sounding distortions are necessary to make it happen.

As an aside, even English and French are slightly different in their grammar of number. The evidence is their expression of fractions. In English you can say "one and a half hours" or "one hour and a half", although the latter form is unusual. In French, only the second form is possible ("une heure et demie"). This form actually implies "one hour and a half hour". In French the mathematical phrase "une et demie" is understood as two numbers added together (1 + ½), as opposed to the

English "one and a half" meaning a single number, namely 1½. I am told that in Français Québécois 1½ can be said as a single number.

We have seen that some languages have verbal grammatical forms for number, and some have adjectival forms. The most common mathematical use is as a noun, and English allows this more easily than most languages. It is interesting to note that some American First Nation languages have a noun-like usage of number in their everyday discourse. Denny (1986) has written on the Ojibway language (which also has verbal numbers) and the Aivilingmiut language which has noun-like grammatical structures for numbers:

one	atausiq	This has no suffix and is a singular noun.
two	marruuk	This has the dual noun suffix –uk.
three	pingasut	This has the plural noun suffix –t.
		It translates as "a group of three".
	pingasuit	This has the adjectival suffix –uit.
		It translates as "three groups".

Hence *pingasut tuktuit* (three caribou) is actually literally translated as a three-group of caribou, or a caribou group-of-three. And *pingasuit tuktuit* is three groups of caribou.

We can imagine that a mathematical discourse involving abstract sets, might be grammatically straightforward in this language.

3.   FUNCTIONING NUMBERS: DHIVEHI

What about Dhivehi, the language of The Maldives? In this language numbers are adjectives or nouns. We know they can be nouns because in Dhivehi nouns are declined, that is, the form of a noun changes when it performs different functions. The suffix on a noun indicates the case. Numbers use the suffix forms for indefinite, non-human nouns (see Table 3-1). Note that the base word for fifteen, *fanara*, is both "the fifteen" and also the form that can be used in the descriptive, adjectival sense: *fanara foiy* (fifteen books).

Dhivehi seems to be like English where number words can be used in a descriptive, adjectival way (as is most common in everyday talk), or as an object in a nominal way (as is most common in mathematics). However it is not quite as simple as that. We need to look more closely at what happens to numbers in English discourse.

Table 3-1. The Word for Fifteen in Dhivehi

Case	Object Word	Number Word	Example
Direct	*fotek*	*fanara*	*Tinek ehkuran **fanara** ehvarey ashaaraya.*
	(a) book	(a) fifteen	Three and **fifteen** are eighteen.
Dative	*fotek-aa*	*fanarayak*	*Hayek **fanarayak** ehkuray*
	to a book	to a fifteen	Add six **to fifteen**.
			*Tinek ehkuran baara ya ehvarey **fanarayak**.*
			Three and twelve are equal **to fifteen**.
Generative	*fotek-ge*	*fanaraige*	*Thireehakee **fanaraige** gunaeh.*
	of a book	of a fifteen	Thirty is a multiple **of fifteen**.
Instrumental	*foteku-n*	*fanarayakun*	*Tinek **fanarayakun** kendeema ehvarey baara ya.*
	from a book	from a fifteen	Three subtracted **from fifteen** equals twelve.
	by a book	by a fifteen	*Saalhees faheh **fanarayakun** gehleema ehvarey tinakaa.*
			Forty-five divided **by fifteen** equals three.
Locative	*foteku-ga*	*fanaraiga*	***Fanaraiga** innanee tin fahek.*
	in a book	in a fifteen	There are three fives **in fifteen**.

The position of the number word before the noun, like a colour or other descriptive word, makes numbers feel like adjectives: red trousers, denim trousers, five trousers. But when we use these in a sentence, we can get differences. Many sentences containing number words are constructed more like noun sentences. Compare the answers to the questions in Table 3-2 and the possible ways they could be answered.

Table 3-2. Number Questions in English (XX indicates an unacceptable form)

Noun Question	Number Question	Adjective Question	Verb Question
What is in the room?	**How many cats are in the room?**	**What are the cats in the room like?**	**What are the cats in the room doing?**
Cats.	Four.	Red.	Sleeping.
There are cats in the room.	There are four cats in the room.	There are red cats in the room.	There are sleeping cats in the room.
There are cats.	There are four.	XX There are red.	XX There are sleeping.
The cats are in the room.	XX The cats in the room are four.	The cats in the room are red.	The cats in the room are sleeping.
They are cats.	XX They are four.	They are red.	They are sleeping.

The similarity with nouns in the third format is because we are permitted to drop the noun, although it is implied. "There are four (cats)". We cannot do this with other adjectives so easily. The final two formats show that using numbers in a sense that answers the implied question "How many?" requires us to use constructions that are different from adjectives, verbs, and nouns:

The trees on the hills are oaks.	No, they are pines.
The trees on the hill are green.	No they are grey.
The trees on the hill are waving in the wind.	No, they are still.
There are three trees on the hill.	No, there are four.

Numbers, in English, have their own grammar that is unlike the grammar of adjectives, verbs or nouns. In various situations their grammar is like the grammar of these other types of words, and this happens in both everyday discourse where they tend to be adjective-like, and in mathematical discourse where they are like nouns:

There are four birds sitting in a tree.	Adjective-like.
There are three boxes of ten bottles, making thirty bottles in all.	Adjective-like.
Add these three pens to those six, and there are nine altogether.	Adjective-like (with 'pens' implied).
Five is a prime number. (Cf. Green is a warm colour).	Noun-like.
Five is a factor of fifteen. (Cf. Green is the complement of red).	Noun-like.
Three times six is eighteen. (Cf. Yellow and blue make green.	Noun-like.
Three sixes are eighteen.	Adjective- and noun-like.

Now in Dhivehi, numbers can be used as adjectives or nouns, so it seems as though this will be well-suited to all the everyday and mathematical constructions above. However in Dhivehi the numbers have the different noun forms. This means not that they are *like* nouns, but that they *are* nouns, and this seriously affects some of the mathematical features of numbers.

First of all consider the difference in English, between "three fives" and "five threes". This is short for saying "three groups of five" and "five groups of three". We know that the total number of objects in these two agglomerations are equal (15), but the way they are structured are different. This is easier to see if we are talking about something in particular: a three-story apartment block with five apartments on each floor is a very different building from a five-story apartment block with three apartments on each floor—although they are both buildings containing fifteen apartments.

In English we can express the multiplication of numbers in several ways:

3×5	5×3
Three fives.	Five threes.
Three multiplied by five.	Five multiplied by three.
Three times five.	Five times three.

In the first of these the number words differ, depending on which way round you say it. The plural form of 'fives' (that only occurs in mathematical talk, not in everyday talk) indicates that this is a 'group of five' and there are three of them, and vice versa. In the second example, the word 'by' indicates that the role of the three is different from the role of the five, despite the form of the words being the same. One number is the instrument of the multiplication of the other. The third example is actually similar, but does not look like it. The 'times' here refers to 'occasions of'. "Three occasions of five" or "three occurrences of five". In this form the 'of' indicates the different role played by each number, but it is suppressed in the conventional form.

In Dhivehi the number words change in the first and second cases because the different role played by the two numbers is embedded in the structure of the word. There is no equivalent to "three times five" in Dhivehi.

3×5	5×3
Tin fahek	Fas tinek
Tinek fahekun gunakururma	Fahek tinekun gunakuruma

An alternative way of saying "three fives" or "five three" uses two old words:

Tin fansa	Fas thirikhu

It seems as though these old forms of five (*fansa*) and three (*thirikhu*) mean something like "groups of five". They have been replaced in modern Dhivehi by *fahek* and *tinek*. But these are interesting also, because there is a choice between the definite and the indefinite forms. "The five" would be *fas*, which is never used in the nominal sense (only in the adjectival one), *fahek* means, literally, "a five", that is, an example of five. Now to create an example of five, to illustrate it, there must be five somethings. So this form of the noun is a version of the implied context that was referred to above in relation to Kankana-ey: its origins at least are in situations where it is possible to add a noun afterwards: "There are six people in the house, five (people) are women." Perhaps this is why, when I asked my informant (a first language Dhivehi speaker) to translate "fifteen is a multiple of five", she responded that she was not sure about it. She had had no trouble with all the arithmetic phrases like "Three plus five is eight" in which additional nouns could more easily be added: "Three birds plus five birds are eight birds". And when I asked for her to translate a sentence that talked about an occurrence of the number five in an equation, "the five tells you the intercept on the axis", she responded that it was difficult.

4.   CONGRUENCE OF LANGUAGE WITH MATHEMATICS

So what? Well this is an example of the difference between everyday language and mathematical language. The symbol form of multiplication (3 × 5) is not the same as the spoken form. The symbol form of multiplication refers only to number, the spoken form also refers to structure. Some people express this as saying that mathematics is about 'pure number'. If 'pure' number is being meant, then 3 × 5 is equal to 5 × 3, i.e. 15. The mathematical term for this reversible feature is commutativity, and it is an important feature of multiplication (and addition) of numbers.

Note that commutativity does not apply to subtraction or division $(3 - 5 \neq 5 - 3$ and $3/5 \neq 5/3)$. In English, for those operations, we retain the prepositions that indicate the role of each number. This is most noticeable when we issue commands. We say "multiply 3 by 5" "add 3 to 5" (roles retained), but also "multiply 3 and 5" "add 3 and 5" (roles lost). For subtraction and division we can only say "subtract 3 from 5" or "divide 3 by 5" (role retained).

So what emerges is that, in this example, English is more aligned to the way things are expressed in mathematics. English, with its own grammar of number, allows us to express the operations of multiplication and addition in the way that they are intended to be understood mathematically; Dhivehi, with numbers fixed as nouns, does not—or, it does not allow it quite so easily.

This is a good opportunity to note something further about the use of numbers in mathematics that is different from our use of numbers in everyday language. The mathematical use of numbers is strictly defined and highly conventional. We have given the example of multiplication, where the symbols 3 × 5 refer to the total (pure) number being represented and not the structure of the groupings. In mathematical language this is "three times five", and is commutative. We have already noted that this is different from any everyday use where actual objects are being discussed, where the structure is part of what is being communicated: 3 floors of 5 apartments; 3 × 5, a piece of timber may be described as 3 by 5 (often written 3 × 5) when what is being referred to is the shape and dimensions of the cross-section. Thus we say that mathematics is removed from reality, it represents the ideal.

Beware! Many have interpreted the use of the word "ideal" in this context as meaning that mathematics represents perfection, the ultimate in abstract thought. That is not what I mean, and nor do I think it is true. I mean that mathematics represents things that are ideas, they come from ideas, they are ideal. But there are many possible ideas, and perfection does not seem like an appropriate word to use for ideas. Ideas are just ideas.

For example, there is another use of "3 × 5" which is quite different from how we usually understand multiplication: this is when it is used to indicate the dimensions of a matrix. A matrix is an array of numbers, and, for most purposes, it is very important to distinguish between a 3 × 5 matrix and a 5 × 3 one (see Fig. 3-1).

$$\begin{pmatrix} 2 & 7 & 4 \\ 0 & -1 & 5 \\ 0 & 1 & -2 \\ -2 & 3 & 4 \\ 1 & -3 & 6 \end{pmatrix}_{5\times 3} \qquad \begin{pmatrix} 2 & 0 & 1 & 1 & -2 \\ -1 & 4 & 0 & 6 & 3 \\ 3 & 3 & -4 & 0 & 1 \end{pmatrix}_{3\times 5}$$

Figure 3-1. Matrices of Different Order

Here the structure is important. When "3 × 5" is read in this context, you should say "three by five"—the preposition is retained and the meaning is "three rows of five entries". This highlights the conventional use of symbols and words in mathematics: the meaning is precise, and natural language is co-opted to express this as best as possible. English is generally quite adaptable to this purpose.

What is the point here? Well, compared with Kankana-ey, Maori, or Dhivehi, English allows the movement of the use of numbers from everyday conversation mode to the mathematical mode quite easily. The grammatical structure of numbers allows them to be used in conjunction with a noun to describe how many, to be used as objects that can be talked about in isolation, and to be used in mathematical senses that are neither of these. This is not true in the other languages for different reasons: in Kankana-ey numbers are more fixed in their descriptive, adjectival mode; in Maori and Tahitian numbers are more fixed in their active, verbal mode; in Dhivehi the numbers are more fixed in their object, nominal mode.

It should be emphasised again that these are not immovable features of these languages. In English there are constructions or word-forms that force an adjectival use, or a verbal use, and so rob numbers of their mathematical features. In the other languages, the mathematical senses of numbers can be expressed, although it may sound a little odd. What is being noted is a privileging of English with respect to the mathematical use of numbers. It is easier, it is closer to NUC-mathematical discourse.

An English-speaker can more easily mathematise quantity into NUC-mathematics. There is no strangeness in the way of talking, so that mathematics-speak, where numbers are concepts to be played with, is natural: there is a congruence between this language and mathematics. Apart from the possible educational benefit of such congruence (and this is discussed in Part III), it is interesting to ask the question "Why does the congruence exist?" One possible answer is that it is simply chance, that English just happens to be more in line with mathematical talk, and therefore if you are an English speaker then mathematical talk will flow naturally. Alternatively, either mathematical ideas have developed the way they have because mathematics developed (and increasingly develops) through English (or Indo-European languages), or, alternatively, that English has developed in the way that it has because it evolved in close contact with mathematics.

I do not believe that it is coincidence that Indo-European languages just happened to be more consonant with mathematics than other languages. Given that mathematics as we know it today has the major parts of its history within an Indo-European environment, this congruence seems to be good evidence that mathematics is a human creation that is influenced by, and influences, other aspects of human creativity in the same environment. Mathematics and language evolved together. They have affected one another in the past, and they are influencing each other in the present.

This first part of the book has presented evidence from different languages of different mathematical conceptions that could lead to different mathematical systems of various kinds. It has also presented evidence that mathematics and language develop together. But developing mathematics is more complicated, of course, than just creating mathematical worlds through language. I do not mean to suggest that language comes first, and that it determines a mathematical world completely. What other factors shape a mathematical world, or, what else has made mathematics the way it is? How much is mathematics determined by the nature of the human mind? By accidents of history? By the needs of society? By already existing mathematics?

We are concerned about what the evidence from language tells us about the relationship between mathematics and human culture and the philosophical status of mathematics. Is it the same everywhere for everyone? What role does mathematics play in our society? How does it grow and what influences the directions of its development? More importantly, where might it be headed in the future?

The second part of the book addresses some of these questions while remaining mostly focused on language and mathematics. On the way, I will explain why mathematicians should be sued for the sinking of the Titanic, how mathematics can enhance your sex life, and why it is not your fault that you had problems adding fractions.

PART II

LANGUAGE AND MATHEMATICS

Chapter 4

THE EVIDENCE FROM LANGUAGE

Abstract: The evidence from language in the preceding chapters is used to question common assumptions about mathematics. The links between mathematics and English language are explored through examples of the use of the words 'open' and 'normal'. The chapter concludes with a summary of the evidence presented so far.

Keywords: language and mathematics, open sets, normal distribution, abstraction, generalisation

In the first part of the book I presented some evidence from different languages together with some mind-games, and suggested that mathematics did not need to develop as it has done. We do not generally consider mathematics as one of several options. I must now, therefore, augment Part I by providing a coherent picture of mathematics that both explains how this can be so, and also fits with our experiences and perceptions of the subject.

Part II fills out the picture of mathematics, giving just such an account of how it originated, how it develops, and what it means. Chapter 5 starts with two examples of a different kind of evidence from language, and then reviews the implications of all the language evidence. In Chapters 6 and 7 the origins and development of mathematics are discussed respectively, and finally I address some philosophical issues. Part III examines educational implications.

1. TWO WORD STORIES: NORMAL AND OPEN

The first story concerns the word *normal*. This word first appeared in the English language in the 16th or 17th centuries, with a mathematical meaning. It occurs, for example, in *The English Euclide*, a translation into English of Euclid's text written in 1696. In that document it meant *right*, as in right-angled, or *rectangular*.

The origin of the word is Latin, starting with the word *norma*, which was the name for a carpenter's square, the pattern that a carpenter used for making exact, right-angled corners, or checking that posts were upright. Today a *norma* is called a set-square, and used in schools and graphic design as well as on building sites. From *norma* came the word *normalis*, meaning "made according to a carpenter's square" and, eventually, by the 15th century, in late Latin, this word had come to mean "in conformity with the rule".

But this is not the end of the story. Someone who is normal is not just someone who conforms with the rules, they are someone like us— well, like me anyway. A normal programme is not the one that follows the rules, it is the one that occurs most frequently. "Most frequently" sounds like probability and statistics—and it is.

Through the 17th and 18th centuries the subject of probability emerged, originating in the interest in gambling in France by the mathematician Blaise Pascal (Hacking, 1975). Indeed, the word *probability* did not occur until 1657. Our word *normal* was still in use mainly as a mathematical term, but also, for example, in the French *école normale*, meaning "by the rule". The *école normale* were schools set up under the Republican foundation in 1794. Then, as late as 1892, *normal* got a new mathematical meaning. It was the name given to the probability distribution that occurs in nature, the Bell Curve as it is sometimes known (see Fig. 4-1).

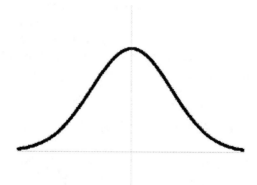

Figure 4-1. The Normal Curve

It was discovered that this distribution modelled what happened for many aspects of human and animal populations: height, weight, performance in mathematics tests, performance in intelligence tests. There seemed to be a general rule governing such data. The mathematical model was therefore named a *normal distribution*, and became a way of categorising. You could now find out whether you were close to the "norm", that is, average height. Young parents are familiar with the consequences. There are charts of baby weight against age, and lines drawn on the chart to indicate the percentiles (see Fig. 4-2).

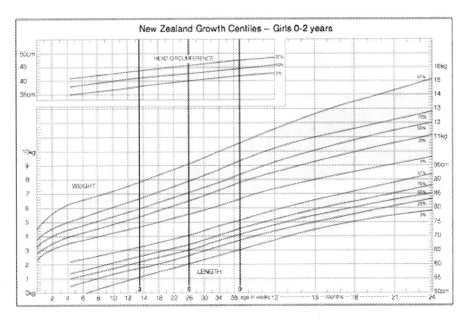

Figure 4-2. Baby Weight & Length Chart
(Reproduced with permission from the New Zealand Ministry of Health *WellChild Tamariki Ora Health Book*, Wellington: Ministry of Health, p. 70)

If your baby comes between these lines, then all is well with the world, grandparents are content, parents don't lie awake worrying about whether they're guilty of mal-nourishing or overfeeding their babies, and the social gathering at the playground is a proud display of ... of a *normal* baby.

That's right. Prior to 1926, when the word *normal* was first used to describe a population, there was no such thing as being normal. Babies just were. Some babies were different from others. Some people were different from others. A few people were a little odd, a little idiosyncratic sometimes, but that was accepted as how the world was. Only in the last 100 years has the concept of normality come to play a major role in how we talk and think about ourselves. As a result of being at the extreme end of the normal distribution, many healthy people have felt guilty about themselves, been put on medication, or been locked up in mental institutions. The sad part about all this is that the mathematics says there will always be some people at the extreme ends of any measurement that is made. Healthy people. Normal people. This is an example of mathematics affecting language and thought.

The second story is about the word *open*.

As a member of a research project I once attended an international conference of mathematical researchers in the field of topology. Topology is that part of mathematics that deals with the mathematical structure of concepts like nearness and continuity. Topologists concern themselves with what it means to say that one number is 'next to' another, for example. Or whether it is possible to have a small finite area that has a boundary that is infinitely long? (The answer is yes!)

Our team was investigating whether the languages that topologists speak affect the way they understand their very abstract subject (Barton, Lichtenberk, & Reilly, 2005; Barton & Reilly, 1999). Breakfast. I sit at a table with three topologists from three different countries. I ask how the name 'Open Set' came into existence. It does not matter, for this story, what an open set is, except to say that it is an absolutely fundamental concept in topology—one of the concepts on which everything else is built. After a short argument about who first used the term, I changed the question to which of the many meanings of the word 'open' was being used here.

"Ah," says the first topologist, "that is easy. Actually any word could have been used, so long as it had an opposite, since it is the relationship between an open set and a closed set that is what is important. Open/closed. Yin/yang. Black/white. It could have been any of these. It is the sense of complementarity that is being expressed."

"What?" queried the second. "I don't think so. The meaning of open in this context is the one used of an international border: anything can pass through, there is no well-defined restriction on what makes the border."

"Oh," mutters the third quietly (he was the junior member of the group), "I always thought that what was meant was the idea of without any boundary at all—like we refer to an open field, the open sea, or an open question."

Fortunately, not being a topologist, my view was neither expected nor important. Which was just as well, because I had imagined that the sense of open being referred to was that of a door. It can be open or shut, it depends what you want to do with it.

Why did the four of us hold four different views—was it language background, prior experiences, or the way we were taught? Is one right and the other three wrong? For the three who are research topologists, does it make a difference to the mathematics they do with open sets that they think about the meaning of open in different ways?

These three topologists each had a different understanding of the word naming the fundamental building block of their research field. It is difficult to imagine that this does not affect the way they research this highly conceptual area of mathematics. This story is an example of the potential for language to affect mathematics.

2.   REVIEWING THE EVIDENCE

These stories do not prove anything, however they are further parts of the picture of the relationship between everyday language and mathematics. A picture of close ties between the two, of each affecting the development of the other, both in the past, and in the present.

Let us be clear about what this part of the book is trying to do, and what it is *not* trying to do. I am trying to paint a consistent picture of mathematics (its nature, its development, how it is connected to human thought) that fits with the evidence from language. What I am *not* trying to do is argue that all other views are wrong—although I will point out, in places, where the evidence from language contradicts some other conceptions of mathematics and its history.

For example, you will not find a denunciation of the Platonist conception of mathematics as an ideal world to be uncovered, nor of the formalist idea that mathematics is simply the setting up of rules and exploring their consequences. I just raise some questions about them. Nor will you find a challenge to the history of mathematics that sees the subject as a single river of development fed by tributaries of contributions from different mathematicians. Rather, I show that an alternative view of a braid of many fibres will also fit the evidence.

There is not room in this book (nor do I have the ability) to disband all other philosophical positions, nor to survey all the writing on the historiography and social influences on mathematics. Rather the book argues that there are some interesting things about the way different people talk mathematically, and that this suggests a picture of mathematics that is somewhat different from many accepted views. But this picture is consistent, and does "make sense" on the evidence available.

Now, let's summarise the evidence, as opposed to recounting anecdotes and flirting with the imagination.

First of all, everyday mathematical talk, that is, general language used to discuss quantity, relationships and space, can be quite different in different languages. For example, with respect to the grammar of quantity, the Polynesian verbal use of numbers, the Kankana-ey adjectival use, and the Dhivehi nominal use are significantly different from the English or Spanish use, a way of speaking that can move between adjectival-like and nominal-like.

Not only are there differences between different languages, but also everyday mathematical talk is changing within each language. For example, the modern Maori grammar of numbers is different from the Maori grammar of numbers before European contact. What causes the change is not clear, and there are likely to be many complex, interacting influences. (Although, in this case, there is evidence that the involvement in language development by those from another language background may have been significant. For example the involvement of missionaries in creating a written form, and the involvement of mathematicians taught in English in establishing a Maori mathematical discourse).

The third point is that the direction of change is towards more similarity. For example, as Dhivehi and Euskera are used in more technical mathematical areas, and as they are used in fields where English or French or Spanish are international mediums of communication, so Dhivehi and Euskera move towards grammatical forms, for example the grammar of numbers, that mirror those of the international language.

Note that these languages were not chosen for discussion *because* the grammar of number was different. It is not true that other non-Indo-European languages were studied, found to be similar to English, and then left out of this book. Each language I encountered had some feature of interest. This suggests that different and changing mathematical grammars are likely to be widespread phenomena.

The examples from the language of space gave evidence that there are linguistically related preferences, or predispositions, to see location and shapes in ways that are conceptually different. Furthermore, these concepts can give rise to formal systems that are different from NUC-mathematics, but perform some of the same functions. If it is true that geometry built up from the way humans conceived of the space and shapes around them, then it has been shown that geometry could have at least started differently, using different basic concepts, and that other graphical representations could have become more familiar.

The examples about the language of number similarly show that the way we describe quantity in NUC-mathematics is not universally familiar, but mirrors that of English and other Indo-European languages—the main languages of mathematical development.

The examples from the language of relationships confirm that categorisation and argumentation do not have universally applicable characteristics. In these examples, unlike those of the alternative geometries, it is not necessarily possible to map one system onto the other. The implication is that categorisation and argumentation are context dependent, and are, in our everyday world, to be judged on their utility within that context. The question for NUC-mathematics is whether it wishes to remain a context only ruled by one form of argumentation, or whether, as a discipline, it can become open to QRS-system investigations ruled by other forms of logic and categorisation?

Another aspect of the evidence is that mathematical processes like formalising, generalising, abstracting, or symbolising are all represented within the examples described. However, since it is everyday language we are talking about, many of the QRS-systems and their mathematical processes are embedded in particular activities, like navigating, weaving, land measurement, or resource allocation. (The study of the mathematical aspects of these systems is known as ethnomathematics (Ascher, 1991; Barton, 1996; Contreras, Morales, & Ramirez, 1998; Monteiro, 2002; Powell & Frankenstein, 1997)). We have seen that at least some of these concepts and systems can be extrapolated in a formal mathematical way to resemble elementary NUC-mathematics. The example of Action Geometry re-maps the relationship between some geometric objects, and appears to deal more easily with some geometric features and less easily with others.

A final note on this review of the evidence in Part I. After investigating mathematical talk in other languages I am left with questions about where the different conceptions came from? Are they linguistic accidents, or do they reflect different physical environments or social activities? Let us move on, then, to discuss the origins of mathematics.

Chapter 5

MUMBLING, METAPHORS, & MINDLOCKS: THE ORIGINS OF MATHEMATICS

Abstract: Devlin's idea of the similarity of mathematics to gossip is explored, and leads
into a discussion of Wittgenstein's ideas on the nature of mathematics. To
this debate is added the recent writings in the cognitive sciences about
mathematics. Examples, such as our conception of fractions, are used to
heighten awareness of the role of communication in mathe-matics, and hence
its dependence on language. Emerging from the discussion is the importance
of metaphor, and the role it plays in the way we talk about and conceive of
mathematics.

Keywords: language and mathematics, Wittgenstein, cognitive science, fractions, metaphor

I will now argue for the major role that language plays in the generation of mathematics. The chapter starts by considering some recent writing that addresses the relationship of the human mind and mathematics. Then it is shown, first, that there could have been other choices made in the way mathematics has grown, second, that these choices are strongly affected by socio-cultural influences, and third, that we create mathematical systems by communicating about them. Hence language is one of the most vital influences on our subject. Finally you will read a description of how this influence occurs.

1.   GOSSIP & MATHEMATICAL TALK

Where does mathematics come from? Is it there, a part of the pre-existing universe, residing in an ideal Platonic world, waiting for us to discover it and come to know it? Or does it grow from human minds reacting to their environment? Or is it both?

Mathematics is just gossip, according to Devlin (2001). He suggests that the human faculty for doing mathematics is the same faculty we use for gossiping. Devlin continues: "the main activity that prepared the human brain for being able to do mathematics was nothing to do with the physical world" (2001, p. 7), rather, it was the human need to keep track of interpersonal relationships. Thus mathematics is gossip, but gossip about abstract relations. I once tested this hypothesis, making a tape of two mathematicians (Mike Newman from Australian National University and George Harras from the University of Queensland) discussing their research. I subjected the transcript to a Barton-Devlin transformation: the nine words that referred to mathematical objects or actions were swapped for nine other words referring to the game of rugby—New Zealand's national game. When the transformed version is read out the conversation is good enough to sound like it makes sense, although a careful examination of the text might lead you to wonder what it really meant (see Table 5-1).

Table 5-1. The Barton-Devlin Transformation

Mathematicians' Gossip Original		Mathematicians' Gossip Transformed
U(3,3)	→	Wellington team
Semigroup	→	Second round
T-system	→	Attacking
Generating pair	→	Throw-in option
Presentation	→	Backline move
Elements	→	Players
Automorphism	→	Player position
Free-group	→	Lineout
Equivalence class	→	Consequence

M	Now, on the U(3,3) you've got the semigroup result which answers something? There's a sense in which I'd like to look at U(3,3) from the, sort of, T-system point of view.	M	Now, on the Wellington team you've got the second round result which answers something? There's a sense in which I'd like to look at the Wellington team from the, sort of, attacking point of view.
G	OK, I think that's a good idea because it is small enough.	G	OK, I think that's a good idea because it is small enough.
M	Exactly. U(3,3) is very small. I mean, we've obviously got some here further, just how many different, essentially different generating pairs has it got? That shouldn't be too difficult to work out.	M	Exactly. The Wellington team is very small. I mean, we've obviously got somewhere further, just how many different, essentially different throw-in options has it got? That shouldn't be too difficult to work out.

Mathematicians' Gossip Original	Mathematicians' Gossip Transformed
G I, I can tell you that I believe I have more than half a dozen. OK, I've got...	G I, I can tell you that I believe I have more than half a dozen. OK, I've got
M Presentations? Or generating pairs?	M Backline moves? Or throw-in options?
G The presentations come from what Eamonn's programme suggests are distinct generating sequences. OK.	G The backline moves come from what Eamonn's programme suggests are distinct throw-in options. OK.
M Ah, yes, but all your generating sequences are either 3-3 or 3-7 aren't they? Orders of two elements. I believe there are two there.	M Ah, yes, but all your throw-in options are either 3-3 or 3-7 aren't they? Orders of two players. I believe there are two there.
G You believe the two generating sequences might all be in the one T-system?	G You believe the two throw-in options might all be in the one attacking plan?
M That needs checking	M That needs checking
G I mean, they are distinct in the sense... well, I don't understand what distinguishes T-systems.	G I mean, they are distinct in the sense... well, I don't understand what distinguishes attacking plans.
M Well automorphisms and automorphisms of the free-group.	M Well player positions and player positions in the lineout.
G I see, so the formal...	G I see, so the formal...
M I mean, the formal definition of a T-system is that it is the equivalence class of generating pairs, in this case generated by the action on generating pairs on the automorphism group or the automorphism group of the free-group. There might only be one of those because the 3-3 and the 3-7 might in fact be got from one another by an automorphism of the free-group. I mean that was your technique for changing from something where you............	M I mean, the formal definition of an attacking plan is that it is the consequence of throw-in options, in this case generated by the action of throw-in options on the player positions or the player positions in the lineout. There might only be one of those because the 3-3 and the 3-7 might in fact be got from one another by swapping players in the lineout. I mean that was your technique for changing from something where you............
G Sure, sure. Yeah. I understand what you're saying. I mean, I also have other generating sets but they have not solved the problem.	G Sure, sure. Yeah. I understand what you're saying. I mean, I also have other throw-in options but they have not solved the problem.

This does not prove Devlin's contention, nor does it illustrate what he really meant, but it does demonstrate that, as far as verbal communication goes, there is not a lot of difference between mathematical and everyday conversation. The difference is mainly technical vocabulary, meaning that the structure of communicating mathematics is the same as the structure of gossip.

Is this where mathematics comes from? Shanker's (1987) interpretation of Wittgenstein is that mathematics is indeed created in our mathematical talk. Under this interpretation, each time we use a mathematical term the concept or relationship is being remade.

For example, when a school pupil first hears and uses the word *prime* then it may have a limited meaning such as "one of the numbers 2, 3, 5, 7, and some others". As the child continues to use the word the meaning will change to "a number generated in Eratosthenes Sieve", and later "a number with no factors other than one and itself". A yet later understanding might be "a positive integer with no factors other than one and itself". But the idea of *prime* is not just its formally correct definition. After understanding Euclid's proof the student will add to their concept the idea of an infinitude of primes, and later the possibility of infinite twin primes.

That description is not just the process of an individual coming to understand a pre-known mathematical concept. It reflects the situation of the community of mathematicians as more and more is known about the concept. Do prime numbers fit with Goldbach's Conjecture (that every even number integer greater than 2 is the sum of two primes—one of the oldest unproven conjectures in mathematics)? Every time some further progress is made on this question, then essentially we are adding to the concept of *prime*, that is, what a prime IS. According to this line of thinking, it makes no sense to assert that a prime either does or does not satisfy Goldbach's Conjecture until the conjecture is proven one way or the other. And once Goldbach's Conjecture is decided, there are many more conjectures about primes waiting to be resolved, and even more waiting to be formed. That is mathematics. So the process of forming the concept of *prime* never finishes. In other words, mathematics is in constant generation through mathematicians' talk. ('Talk' in this sense includes writing, of course. Perhaps we should say 'communication').

Devlin's idea that mathematics is generated in each of us through our ability to gossip, and Shanker's version of Wittgenstein that mathematics is constantly generated during mathematical communication, are both ideas that fit with the evidence from language. The Realist version of mathematics, that there is a Platonic world we come to know, or even the quasi-empiricist one that we experience mathematics, do not fit so well with the observations that numbers and shapes are conceived as actions in one culture and as things in a different cultures. If mathematics is generated with language, then such differences are to be expected.

Similarly, a formalist conception, that mathematics results inevitably from the establishment of a set of rules, does not easily accept the consequences of different forms of argumentation and logic.

Let us go back to Devlin's idea that the human genetic disposition for language is exactly what was required for humans to do and develop mathematics: "thinking mathematically is just a specialised form of using our language facility" (2001, p. 4). This statement coincides with our evidence from language. The language facility is extraordinarily varied, however, and so the possible specialised usages of it to talk about quantity or relationships or space are also varied. This is another way of saying that, if mathematics is generated through our language facility, then it is culturally shaped in the same way as language.

But if mathematics arises from language, then we must consider mathematics in the same way we consider language. Different concepts are expressed in different languages, and some concepts are extremely difficult, some say impossible, to translate between languages. The implication is that different quantitative, relational, and spatial concepts may also not be easily transformed into each other. The language investigations reported in Part I confirm this.

Sometimes Devlin seems to abandon the implications of his main hypothesis: for example suggesting that "our capacity for mathematical thought evolved" (2001, p. 7), when it was mathematics that evolved (just as language has evolved) not our capacity for it; or describing mathematics as tracing a single, almost inevitable, evolutionary path, when the path is not inevitable if it is linked to the development of language. But Devlin is not the only person to hesitate at the brink of the consequences of describing social, linguistic, and cultural origins of mathematics.

2.   COGNITIVE SCIENCE CONTRIBUTIONS

Dehaene (1997) discusses the origins of arithmetic in our minds, making an approach from cognitive science. Actually, Dehaene's work does not discuss how the mind creates mathematics, as Devlin notes (2001, p. 21), but rather how mathematics exists in the mind. However it does contain some evidence about language that is relevant to our discussion.

He describes elementary "number sense" in very young children, prior to language. Young children recognise two objects as different from one object, and look around for the second if one is taken away. Young children also recognise subtle features—their mother's faces as opposed to their aunt's, for example—so we should not be surprised that they detect the presence or absence of objects. The question is whether this represents *number*. People seem confused between the cognitive, perceptive ability (that I would call *quantity*), and the mathematical concept developed as part of the system of mathematics (that I would call *number*).

It is in the communication of the experience of *quantity* that the concept of *number* is formed, and this occurs with the development of language.

Dehaene's book presents the evidence for this, although he only talks about English. He claims that there are two keys to humans' understanding of number beyond three: counting and using symbols. He describes how a three year old can count, say, six objects, but when asked immediately afterwards how many toys she or he has, may reply with any number. My explanation from a language point of view is <u>not</u> that the child is confusing the process of counting with the abstract concept of number. Rather, the process of counting is a language learning "game" where a sequence of words is learned in conjunction with one-to-one association. The child, however, does not have a concept of number because that concept *is* the answer to the question "How many?"—it is a different kind of thing than counting. The child is in the process of learning the correct communicative response to that particular question, he or she knows that the answer is a number word, but has not got the number concept by which the correct number word is identified.

The next piece of evidence given by Dehaene clearly demonstrates such reasoning. Children younger than three understand how to use number words in English in a descriptive way that is different from how adjectives are used. [.. also check in Dehaene not just Devlin] They know to say "three little sheep" and not "little three sheep", for example. They know that numbers refer to groups of objects and not to characteristics of them like colour or texture. Now, we know that different languages use number words in different ways. Polynesian languages use numbers verbally in everyday use, and the Aivilingmiut Inuit language uses numbers as nouns in everyday use. It is reasonable to assume that young children from these cultures can also use number words correctly in their language. There is nothing universal about the adjectival use of numbers. This must be a *learned* behaviour. So the way that quantity is expressed, is learned, not innate or determined by our genes. It is the expression of the quantity sense, as a number system, that constitutes mathematics.

There is considerably more about arithmetic and language in Dehaene's book, including wonderful experiments that show the exact nature of this link, and, in Devlin's book, this is extended to other mathematical activity like logical reasoning. Between them they present considerable evidence that doing mathematics is language-based. For example, Devlin attributes to number-word characteristics of the Mandarin language the advantage of Chinese children over European ones in elementary arithmetic. (Yet Devlin explicitly denies the language-dependence of doing mathematics (2001, p. 70)).

Cognitive science is now able to map brain activity corresponding to human tasks. Evidence from MRI scans tells us that, when counting or performing simple arithmetic, there is more activity in the left parietal lobe of the brain, whereas language activities activate the frontal regions more. (Note that all mental activities distribute over large portions of the brain and some areas can replace others: there is no "language part" or "counting part").

More light is shed on this by an experiment Dehaene and colleagues performed that involved monitoring the brain during some arithmetic activity. Part of the activity involved approximation tasks, and part required exact answers. The former activated the parietal lobes more, the exact answers activated the frontal lobes more. The left parietal lobe is also associated with finger movement, and my explanation is that that part of the brain is important for quantity sense, things like estimating size and counting. Converting this information into a system that can deal with quantity (that is, doing arithmetic) requires the same region that is associated with language.

A comparison might be the sense of touch. It is one thing to feel the texture of something, to have, and register, the experience of it. It is quite another thing to communicate this feeling, to compare it with the texture of other things, to categorise the way different things feel. This is the difference that I want to emphasise between the quantity sense on one hand, and arithmetic as a system that is part of mathematics on the other.

Before moving past cognitive science, let us consider some of the cases that Brian Butterworth describes in his book *The Mathematical Brain* (1999). He describes a woman who had a stroke that destroyed her "numerical" ability, but who retained her reasoning and language abilities. It was her *quantity* sense that was lost: she could not count or estimate the number of objects beyond four, she could not *recite* the number words beyond four. Another woman had a damaged left parietal lobe and also could not count, nor did numbers have any meaning. She could learn arithmetic facts as language, but she could not use them. Again it is not arithmetic that was lost, but the quantity sense. Arithmetic is the system that allows us to use the quantity sense. However, without that sense, arithmetic is meaningless. The other examples of intelligent people who have no "number sense" can similarly be re-understood as having a difficulty not with number or arithmetic, but with their sense of quantity.

A further set of examples describes people who can read number symbols, but not number words, or vice versa. This is a separate issue concerning symbolic representation, not quantity sense or arithmetic systems, but it highlights the interrelationships of different faculties that go together to make mathematical activity possible. The same thinking can be used to explain the New Scientist (19th February, 2005, p. 18) report about brain-damaged patients who could no longer speak, and who could not distinguish between "the boy chased the girl" and "the girl chased the boy", but could nevertheless distinguish between $7 - 2$ and $2 - 7$.

The three books discussed each deal with cognition and arithmetic, or, in Devlin's case, wider mathematics. Devlin and Dehaene both provide more evidence and argument for a close connection with language in the formation of mathematics. The evidence from cognitive science does not necessarily deny this when a distinction is made between the experience of quantity and the mathematical system that formalises that experience (number and arithmetic). Symbols, one way of recording this system, is another matter again.

3. FRACTION SYSTEMS

I now illustrate a key aspect of the formalisation of the experience of quantity through language, that is, the role of human agency in the process. If we are to argue that mathematics is a human creation, then we must show that in the origins of mathematics humans had the opportunity to create it differently that they did.

This can be shown through the formalisation we know as fractions, the *bête noir* of many a child (or adult). Here is a fictional story, a story, perhaps, that will remind you of your own mathematics class-room experiences.

A Story of Four Parts

A teacher of a class of young children sets the following problem:

$$\frac{1}{4} + \frac{3}{8} =$$

Like a good modern teacher, she asks the children to work in groups of four, talking to each other about what they are doing. Relative quietness for a while, some gentle discussion, and then, slowly rising in intensity, one group start arguing, each of the four students trying to convince the others in the group about something. The teacher is confident that she has taught the addition of fractions well, and that at least one of the group knows how to do it, but eventually it becomes clear that none of the children are giving way on their point of view. So she stops the class and invites the students to come to the board and for each of them to write down what they think is the right answer. The result is the following:

Johnny

$$\frac{1}{4} + \frac{3}{8} = \frac{4}{12}$$

Mere

$$\frac{1}{4} + \frac{3}{8} = \frac{5}{16}$$

Tom

$$\frac{1}{4} + \frac{3}{8} = \frac{3}{32}$$

Phillipa

$$\frac{1}{4} + \frac{3}{8} = \frac{5}{8}$$

The teacher is a little bemused, but thinks she sees the problems, so she invites the students to go back to the board and show their working. They are all happy to oblige. This is what Johnny wrote:

$$\frac{1}{4} + \frac{3}{8} = \frac{1+3}{4+8} = \frac{4}{12}$$

The teacher can see that Johnny has certainly done something that is reasonable, even if it is wrong. In order to try to get him to see this she draws two circles, one cut into eighths and one into twelfths, and asks him to shade in both $\frac{3}{8}$ and the result of the sum, $\frac{4}{12}$. It is clear that $\frac{4}{12}$ is smaller than $\frac{3}{8}$.

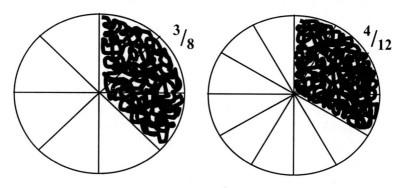

"How can you add something to $\frac{3}{8}$ and get something smaller?" asks the teacher. "That is exactly what I want to know," Johnny responds, "because yesterday you gave us a test. There were two parts, A and B. In part A there were four questions, and I got one right. My Mum and Dad were disappointed in me because I only got a quarter of them right. But in Part B, I got three out of eight questions right. I did much better, and you said that all questions were worth one mark. So how come when I add my test marks together, one quarter plus three eighths, I get less? I've done the addition correctly, altogether I got four questions right out of twelve questions in total."

Johnny, it was apparent, certainly could add! (Kline, 1973). The teacher was bemused by this unexpected justification. "Well I'm afraid that that is not how we do fractions," she said, "test marks aren't real fractions. Let's look at Mere's working," she added hurriedly, to give herself time to regain her composure. Johnny subsided muttering about "real fractions", and the teacher felt unsatisfied with the answer she had given. However, she was sure about Mere's mistake. Here is what Mere had written:

$$\frac{1}{4} + \frac{3}{8} = \frac{2}{8} + \frac{3}{8} = \frac{2+3}{8+8} = \frac{5}{16}$$

"Very good, Mere," the teacher started, "you know that when adding fractions you need to write the fractions with the same denominator. Yes, one quarter is the same as two eighths. And now you add. But why did you add both the top line and the bottom line?" Mere sensed she had done something wrong, but was unclear what or why. All she could respond with was "Because it gave me the right answer." Again the teacher resorted to circles, and Mere's drawing showed that $\frac{5}{16}$ was even smaller than $\frac{4}{12}$. "But it *is* the right answer," insisted Mere. "I know this sum. My Dad is one quarter Maori, and my Mum is three eighths Maori. I am their child, and I am five sixteenths Maori." Her tone challenged the teacher to disagree, but the teacher knew better. Not only was she sure that this descendent of a Maori chief would have her genealogical facts right, she quickly realised that $\frac{5}{16}$ was indeed the average of $\frac{1}{4}$ and $\frac{3}{8}$, the calculation that was required to work out Mere's Maori descent. The teacher was beginning to see the problem now. "Well," she said, "you're right when it comes to adding genealogies, but that is not how mathematicians agree to add fractions. When you get to a higher class you will see that adding genealogies is really taking the average of two fractions, not adding fractions, although it seems as though that is what you should do." Mere, mollified but still mystified, also subsided and the teacher went on to Tom. This is what he had written:

$$\frac{1}{4} + \frac{3}{8} = \frac{1}{4} \times \frac{3}{8} = \frac{1 \times 3}{4 \times 8} = \frac{3}{32}$$

Well that, at least, was pretty clear. Tom had multiplied (correctly) when he should have added. Surely she would not have to resort to showing that $\frac{3}{32}$ was an even smaller section of the circle and could not possibly be the result of adding two larger pieces together. But, wary now, and remembering that he had argued just as vociferously as Johnny and Mere, she gave him a chance to explain himself. "I am only doing what you told me," Tom piped up. "You always said to us that the word 'and' means addition. I was watching my older sister do her maths last night, and she was working with probabilities. Exactly this sum came up in a problem. It was this. 'A boy enters the cafeteria. He knows that the probability of getting the meal he wants is one quarter, and the probability of sitting next to his friend is three eighths. What is the probability that he gets the meal he wants AND sits next to his friend.' My sister said we had to multiply to get the answer, so that's what I did. I know the answer is right because we checked it in the back of the book. It also makes sense because the chance that both things will happen is going to be very small."

The teacher starting wondering about the effect of all this on the class who had a test coming up and needed to get the method for adding fractions correct if New Zealand was to hold its head high in the international league tables. But she finally addressed the real issue. "Well, you have surprised me, Johnny, Mere, and Tom. Each of you have given me a situation in which your method of adding fractions is the right one. And they are all different. But they are correct ways of combining fractions only in that situation. The thing is, the situations you have chosen are not the one that is most common in mathematics, and the one that mathematicians call "addition". There is another situation that gives us another way to combine fractions, and that is the one that we have to learn." She turned to Phillipa, "Show us …". But then she noticed that Phillipa was quietly crying, tears dropping onto her exercise book. Now Phillipa was her star pupil, she was the one that the teacher knew would get the sum right, and who had been expected to demonstrate to the others in her group the correct method. Indeed, her working showed exactly that:

$$\frac{1}{4}+\frac{3}{8} = \frac{2}{8}+\frac{3}{8} = \frac{2+3}{8} = \frac{5}{8}$$

Phillipa refused to move. "I'm the only one who got it wrong," she sobbed. "I thought I had learned the correct method, but when I look at it, it makes no sense. I can understand writing one quarter as two eighths, but there is no reason to add only the top numbers and not the bottom ones. That doesn't seem right. Why would you do that? All the others have got a reason for what they did, and I don't." Phillipa had learned the method the teacher had taught the class, but had no example to illustrate it, and no rationale for her technique. She was bright enough to understand the methods the others had used, and they made sense for her. Her own method made no sense, and no matter what the teacher said, Phillipa was too deeply embarrassed to be comforted. The teacher decided to leave for another day the explanation about the eights being the name of the fraction, or, cutting up pizzas into eighths and adding the pieces. She felt the wave of relief as the bell rang, and went off to rethink what it was that she was doing in mathematics.

What can we say about this story, or, rather, what can this story say to us about where mathematics comes from? First of all let us put aside the educational implications of this. What is it that the teacher might rethink? This will be discussed further in Part III of this book, but briefly, she may think again about how mathematics is presented to her children, she may be more careful about using the words "right" and "wrong", preferring rather to mention conventions more often, or to explain the context of mathematical concepts.

Second, let us note again the importance of language in this story. "And" is loosely associated with addition, just as "times" and "by" are loosely associated with multiplication. But these are only loose associations, and the word "and" is used in four different mathematical senses here. Everyday communication is not the same as mathematical communication, where there are conventions about the meanings of conjunctions and prepositions as well as technical terms and symbols. These conventions need to established anew when languages like Dhivehi, Euskera or Maori are being developed for mathematics classroom discourse if they have never been used in this technical way before. It is not an easy matter to translate "by" in the following sentences:

> Increase 12 by 3
> Increase 12 by three times
> Increase 12 by an amount of 3
> Increase 12 by a factor of 3

But what about mathematics? What does the story tell us about where mathematics comes from? The four ways of "adding" (that is, combining) fractions are all valid in their contexts. If we look at this from the point of view of formal mathematics, there is an explanation for what is going on, even a name for the mathematical result in each case: respectively weighted average, arithmetic average, union of probabilities, and sum. Only the last is the result of "addition" in the arithmetic sense equivalent to adding 3 + 8. However this is a *post hoc* explanation. What we want to know is how formal mathematics came to be like that? How is it that the mathematics we learn in school privileges one of these four ways (contexts) for combining fractions and not the others? For many people, combining probabilities, or combining genealogies, or combining test scores, is at least as frequent an out-of-school activity as combining pieces of pizza or its equivalent.

The point is that we *choose* what to make into a system. We experience aspects of our quantitative (relational or spatial) world and then create systems to handle them, to explain them, to communicate them. This is where mathematics comes from. Which ones do we choose, and how do we create the systems to deal with them? The answers to these questions are complex, of course, but the evidence seems to indicate that we choose the features that are important socially and culturally, and that we create mathematical systems by communicating about them. Language plays a key role in both of these. The evidence does not lead us to believe that the features of our world had a prior order of importance that human minds are forced to follow, nor does it support the idea that the systems were forced to take the form that they actually have.

It is also true that mathematical reasons contribute to the choices made when creating new mathematics—but this comes into play once some mathematics is established, and so is more appropriately considered in the development, rather than the origins, of the subject.

4.   HISTORICAL EVIDENCE

We find further evidence of choices in the formation of mathematics in the history of the subject. Here are two examples, one is a famously documented episode from the 17th century, the other is current history-in-the-making.

An important episode in the development of analysis occurred in the first half of the 19th century as mathematicians were trying to make analysis rigorous. A Frenchman called Cauchy developed a particular concept of what 'continuous' meant mathematically. That is, he described what he thought were the mathematical characteristics of a curve that had no gaps in it, no matter how tiny. With this description he developed some theorems. A German called Weierstrauss, developed another idea of continuous based on always being able to find a point on the curve that was within a specified distance (no matter how small) of another point. There developed a long argument between these eminent mathematicians and their supporters, because, if you used the Weierstrauss system, then it was easy to see that Cauchy's theorems were mistaken. But for thirty years Cauchy refused to acknowledge his mistake.

Two important commentaries on this debate by Lakatos (1978, Chpt. 3) and Robinson (1966) describe it in a different light (see Barton, 1996, Section 5.4, for further discussion of this example). They see the 'argument' as two groups talking past each other because they held two different conceptions of the continuum (that is, the line containing all numbers). Cauchy's work was true for those who held his view of the number line, Weierstrauss' work was true for those who subscribed to his description. It happened that one of these (Weierstrauss') came to be more accepted, and modern analysis is based on that view. But there is a minor branch of mathematics (non-standard analysis) which (it is claimed by its originator, Robinson) arises from the Cauchy conception. A choice was made for what mainstream mathematics has become—it could have been otherwise.

The second example is a contemporary one. Statisticians argue about two competing definitions of the concept of probability. The very existence of this debate effectively demonstrates that the mathematical creation of a concept is quite subjective. Probability is assumed to be understood by everyone in general discourse, although any mathematics teacher will know that it is an extraordinarily difficult topic to teach effectively. Probability, as a mathematical idea, has origins in the 17th century. The original idea, now known as the Frequentist view, is based on what happens in the long-run. That is, if the same event happens over and over, the proportion of times the desired event occurs is its probability. Tossing a coin, or throwing dice exemplify this state of events: after many tosses a fair coin will come down heads 50% of the time, and you will throw a number less than three on a die one third of the time. Many pupils have tossed hundreds of coins or dice in their mathematics lessons to get this idea.

But there is another view called Bayesian probability. In this conception probability is seen as the prior knowledge we have about a one-off situation, and this prior knowledge may change before the event occurs. A cricket match is a good example: from experience and past history we make some estimates of what is likely to happen, but as the game draws closer and we see what the pitch is like, or who is injured, we may revise our estimate for this particular match. With the help of TV graphics, we even analyse the progress of the game and keep revising our estimate until the result is known.

When a statistician is faced with a problem that involves probability, the way he or she works depends on which conception of probability is used, and, in many cases, the 'best' decision differs in each case (see Berger, 1980, for several examples). Most working statisticians can use whichever approach they think is most appropriate, but there remains a debate (Meyer & Collier, 1970) about which is the proper meaning of probability. If one of these conceptions, or a development of it, comes to dominate the whole field of theoretical statistics (and some university statistics departments are already dominated by one approach), then a choice will have been made between two different mathematical constructions of one human experience.

Another example of choice will be familiar to those who were in school in UK, USA, New Zealand or Australia during the 1970s when the geometry syllabus changed from a Euclidean approach to one based on transformations.

5.   SOCIAL INFLUENCE ON CHOICE

So, the evidence from other languages, from the structures of mathematics, and from the historical development of the subject gives us examples of choices being made as mathematics is created. I now argue that the factors that determine those choices are primarily social and cultural. What is the evidence?

One of the key pieces of corroborating evidence is that NUC-mathematics has a correspondence with those languages (mainly Indo-European) in which it was developed. Therefore either the languages (and hence cultures) of its development affected mathematics, or mathematics affected those languages, or a bit of both.

Many others have written about the formation of new branches of mathematics emerging from social influences. For example, the requirements of war have led to mathematical developments, from the inventions of Archimedes to the present day laser-guided systems. It is no accident that much funding for science and mathematics research has been controlled by the American Military institutions. Well-documented are the ways in which economic change has led to new mathematical problems (for example, Swetz, 1987); the evolution of mathematicians early work from their origins as astronomers and land measurers (for the purposes of calculating taxes) (for example, Swetz, 1974); and even social fashions leading to new mathematical fields, for example gambling in 17th century France (David, 1962). More importantly, the very way in which mathematics takes place has social origins. Mathematical proof in its present form has evolved through origins in Greek argumentation (Lizcano, 1993; Fang & Takyama, 1975), and much has been written about alternative forms of mathematical argumentation emerging from the environments of the Arab, Indian, and Chinese worlds (Berrgren, 1986, 1990; Joseph, 1992, 1994; Khare, 1988; Tambiah, 1990).

Devlin (2001, p. 244ff) describes how language is involved in the creation of mathematics. He argues that the abstraction ability that enables us to gossip (that is, our language facility) is exactly what is required to create the 'mathematical houses' in which mathematicians mentally reside. The processes and structures of language are the same as those needed for building the houses of mathematical systematisation.

Devlin talks about (2001, p. 118ff) "levels" of abstraction as part of the language facility used when creating mathematics. For example, the third level of abstraction corresponds to objects of thought that may be real objects heard about but never encountered, or imaginary variants or combinations of real objects, like a unicorn as a horse with a single horn. Level four abstraction is where mathematics takes place and the objects of abstraction "have no simple or direct link to the real world" other than that they are abstracted from it. Devlin is not postulating that these levels exist, he just finds them useful as a way of thinking—I do too.

The question that Devlin does not approach, but which interests me about this model, concerns the choices that are necessary during the abstraction. Devlin claims that it is the patterns, particularly the structural patterns that are of interest. However our language evidence tells us that there is more than one structural pattern in any reasonably complex real world situation. The claim being made in this book is that humans select (often unconsciously) which pattern to abstract using many criteria, and not all (not even most) of the criteria used are mathematical. That is, we do not consciously choose what to abstract by evaluating what is most general, or most useful, or most like existing mathematical structures (although all those may come into play), but the socio-cultural environment in which we live has a hand in making the choices for us. We are affected in these choices by the sorts of questions being asked around us, the things we have been doing recently, the way our language highlights some things and not others, the subjects of interest to our immediate community, or the tools or symbol systems we already have at our disposal.

6.   THE ROLE OF COMMUNICATION

We have provided evidence that there are choices in the creation of mathematics, and we can see social and cultural factors affecting those choices. What about the evidence for concluding that we create mathematical systems by communicating about them, and hence that language is a vital influence?

The main evidence that mathematics is created from communication lies in the correspondence between mathematics and language: features of mathematical systems coincide with features of communication. For example, we are familiar with the different bases of number words in different languages. This topic has been studied extensively since linguistic anthropology began, and many collections of number words exist (for example, Lean, 1995; Menninger, 1969). Indeed, conclusions about the origins and migrations of people have been made through the linguistic links of number words and their bases (Lean, 1995; Owens, 2001).

Our number system is base ten, as is our language. Or is it? What about *eleven* and *twelve*, and words like *dozen* and *score*? Remember that the English monetary system used to be pounds, shillings and pence: twelve pence in a shilling, twenty shillings in a pound. Other Indo-European languages also have examples of other bases: French *quatre-vingt* = four twenty = 80. Dhivehi has an older base twelve system that has nearly disappeared in favour of the modern base ten system: *dolas* = 12; *dolas ekek* = 13; *dolas dek* = 14; ..., *fassihi* = 24; *fassihi ekek* = 25; and so on. In ancient Babylonian times there was a strong base 60 system, and from it we have the number of minutes in an hour, and the number of degrees in a circle (6 x 60 = 360).

This does not mean that language determined mathematics, it seems more like mathematics affected language. Surely the old

English monetary system gave us the special words for base 12 or base 20? This conclusion is likely since the Sanskrit origins of Indo-European languages are more purely base ten, and German and English have special words for eleven and twelve when Sanskrit does not. Did ancient mathematicians measuring stars and angles generate the base sixty system in Babylonia? In 2003 the History of Mathematics web discussion group had a long debate about whether this was the case. Such mathematics to language movement is happening now, where the base ten measuring system generates words like micro- (a micro-metre is 0.000 001metres) and mega- (a megaton is 1 000 000 tons), words now used in everyday language separately from their original measurement system connotations: micro-computer and mega-burger.

What is more likely (based on language evidence) is that mathematics and language developed together. Against the micro- and mega- examples, we should look more closely at base ten. It seems likely that base ten number systems (which do dominate world languages) arose from the number of fingers humans happen to have. They were (they still are) our first and most used counting tools. But mathematically, ten is not such a good number to have as the base of your counting system. Twelve would be much more sensible as it has more factors: 1, 2, 3, 4, 6 and 12 all divide exactly into twelve, whereas ten can only be divided by 1, 2, 5 and 10. This means that more fractions can be expressed easily in a base twelve system. For example, the very common fraction one third has a decimal (base ten) representation with an infinite number of digits. Very inconvenient. If we had a base twelve system, the less common one fifth would be an infinite series of numbers after the point, and halves, thirds, quarters and sixths would all be single digit numbers after the point. So why is the dominant number system in mathematics base ten? The case that language as an expression of social practice determined the mathematical system seems very clear here.

There are other examples. We most commonly think of angles as measured in degrees, where there are 360° in a full turn, or 90° in a right angle. Clearly the right angle has always been very important in our world, and we can imagine that there must always have been words for things that are exactly upright or square—remember the origins of the word *normal*. The base ten number system (derived from our fingers) combined with the idea of a right angle (derived from upright objects in our environment), gives an angle measurement system where there are 100 units in a right angle. This unit is called a *grad* and is still in common use amongst surveyors in some countries. Most calculators can be switched into three modes for angle: degrees, radians, and grads (D, R, and G). The unit *grad*, of course, is related to our words *gradient* (meaning slope), and *gradual* (meaning gently, originally, a gentle slope), with origins in the French *grade* = step.

If base ten systems are natural, why are angles not commonly measured in grads? Why are degrees used instead?

We have established that features of NUC-mathematics coincide with features of language. But not all languages have the same features, although the ones that were mainly used during the development of mathematics do have those features strongly. Remember that it is not just the surface features of mathematics that coincide with the particular languages of its development. For example, the objectification of number and shape, and the language of rational argumentation originating in Greek philosophy are both language-specific attributes.

Another piece of evidence from language that supports the hypothesis that mathematics develops through communication is that the meanings of most fundamental words in mathematics are not the same now as they have been in the past. The exact meanings of 'number', 'geometry', 'proof', 'angle', 'multiplication', and most other mathematical terms have changed and will probably change again. Let us look at the changes in the first three of these.

Number, in Greek times, was associated with lengths of lines, and it even changed within the span of Greek mathematical thought (Klein, 1968). Numbers were related to the geometric measurement of length. Originally it was thought that if you had any two lengths then you could always find a smaller length that would divide into both of them exactly (see Fig. 5-1). For example two lengths of 24 units and 56 units can both be divided into smaller lengths of 8 units. It was believed that this was always possible, although the smaller unit might be a very, very tiny length. For example two lengths of one quarter of a unit and one fifth of a unit can be divided into smaller lengths of one twentieth of a unit.

Figure 5-1. Dividing Two Lengths

Then the Greeks discovered that if you draw a square, say with sides of length one unit, and then you draw the diagonal of that square, then there was no small length that would divide exactly into both the diagonal and the side (Lasserre, 1964). There was a crisis in Greek philosophy as a result. It is said that, when this was first discovered, it was kept secret for some time because the result was so disastrous. This was the first *irrational* number, that is, a number that cannot be represented by a fraction. All numbers had previously been thought to be expressible as ratios of two numbers (that is, fractions). They were *rational*. Now here was a number that could not be written as a ratio. The Greeks thought that they were going mad—and there is the origin of the everyday meaning of *irrational*: the human condition of being without sense or reason. One is irrational if one does not agree to obvious, logical conclusions—just as these numbers did not obey the reasoned, logical philosophies of the Greeks of that time.

Nowadays irrational numbers are accepted as part of our number world, we know there are even more of them than there are rational numbers. We accept irrationals as part of the meaning of the word *number*. Together, these two groups of numbers are known as the *Real Numbers*.

Next, mathematicians, in response to the needs of algebraic calculations, devised negative numbers. But many European mathematicians would not accept negative numbers as proper numbers (Kline, 1980), a situation that went on for a couple of hundred years. We now take them as normal. After that came complex numbers— numbers that include the square root of −1. These were first considered by Cardano (in 1545), but not as numbers so much as a convenient fiction that allowed the solution of some cubic equations. Euler, (in 1777) introduced the notation i to stand for $\sqrt{-1}$, but again it took until 1833 when Hamilton described in detail the number system implied by these numbers before complex numbers were accepted as part of what is meant by the word number. Then it was found that there were still some 'numbers' missing from this collection. They are the transcendental numbers—and there are more of them than all the other kinds of numbers! Described by Leibnitz (in 1674) and Euler (in 1733), transcendental numbers are numbers that cannot be the solution to a polynomial equation. In 1844 Liouville was the first to prove a number was transcendental, and it is now known that π and e are both of this kind.

But the development of the meaning of the word number is not just a matter of adding new types of numbers. In 1958 Dedekind redefined what is meant by the real numbers. He made the concept more rigorous by describing it as a collection of sets of rational numbers, hence, it might be said, returning sanity (rationality) to the idea of number. It is unlikely that we have the end of this story yet.

What about the changing meanings of the word *geometry*? Let us focus on its meaning in Europe only (Eves, 1969). Geometry was originally the mathematical study of land measurement (hence *geo-land*, *-metry measurement*). In France surveyors are still called *geometers*. The Greeks then developed their more abstract study of lines and angles into a method, by which one started with axioms and then deduced a system of results. Geometry became this method, although it was still seated in the human 3-dimensional conception of space. Descartes, Bernoulli, and others, in the 17th century developed coordinate systems that allowed geometrical figures and algebra to be linked. Space came to be regarded as a set of points. And in the 18th century Monge, Poncelet and others developed projective geometry as the study of representing 3-dimensional objects in two dimensions. Monge, and later Gauss and then Bernoulli developed differential geometry which used the (then new) ideas of the calculus to investigate the properties of curves and surfaces and how they are related to the total geometric structure. These geometries moved, in various ways, away from the Greek meaning of geometry, but the link with our conception of space remained until the 19th century when Gauss, Bolyai, Lobachevsky, then Klein and others, first doubted, then proved, that one of the basic Greek postulates that had been taken as self-evident could be denied and a consistent geometric system would still result. Non-Euclidean geometries broke open the understanding that "had for two millennia been bound by the prejudice of tradition to the firm belief that Euclid's system was most certainly the only way geometrically to describe physical space" (Eves, 1969, p. 185). The breakthrough allowed geometry to metamorphise once again in the 19th century. Through the development and generalisations of topology, geometry became the study of abstract spaces, where a space is simply a set of objects. What was a study of physical space is now so abstract that "the boundary lines between geometry and other areas of mathematics have become very blurred … . It is essentially only the terminology and the mode of thinking involved that makes the subject 'geometric' " (Eves, 1969, p. 191).

And *proof*? One example will suffice. The moment that mathematicians decided to accept the proof of the Four Colour Theorem (Appel & Haken, 1977; Appel, Haken & Koch, 1977), and it was not done without a fight, then the idea of proof changed. The long-held concept that a proof was a series of steps that could be checked one after the other by another mathematician had to go. Why? This theorem is the one that says that any map can be coloured using just four colours without two regions of the same colour sharing a common boundary. The way it was proved was to try it out on all possible maps. The problem is that there are quite a few of them. In fact a football stadium of mathematicians working for the known history of mathematics so far would still not have completed the task (Gardner, 1966). So how was it done? Once a way of determining all possible maps was found, the rest was routine. A little complicated perhaps, but routine enough to be programmed onto a computer, and the computer only took a matter of hours to sort it through. The computer reported that no map was found needing more than four colours, *ergo*, theorem proved—or is it? Is agreement amongst the mathematicians of the correctness of the computer programme the same thing as agreement amongst mathematicians of each step of a proof?

So even the idea of proof changes. As mathematicians discuss with each other, express their mathematical ideas, the very meanings of the words they use have to change. This is just another way of saying that the mathematics emerges from its communication.

Let it be acknowledged that this is not quite the same as saying that the communication makes the mathematics. Perhaps all that happened is that the first time a mathematical idea got talked about the participants to the conversation did not get it all right, and that subsequent conversations are needed to sort it out properly—this is the change we are seeing.

The evidence of changing mathematical meanings is, however, consistent with an interpretation that mathematical communication creates new conceptions, or reveals new ideas needing systematisation. Devlin describes his mathematical activity as like building a house (2001, p. 120ff). Then he says:

Notice that, once the house has been built and the instructions and plans have been stored away, there is no more need for language. I simply *live* in the house. Language is required only if some problem sends me back to the plans, or if I want to remodel or purchase a new item. And, of course, I need language if I want to describe to someone else how I built the house or why I arranged the furniture the way I did.

In the light of other evidence, this becomes a lovely, if implicit, statement of the use of language in mathematical creation.

Where does mathematics come from? The evidence from language points to the conclusion that mathematics arises after, not before, human activity. The development of mathematical language is consistent with the idea that mathematical concepts, objects, and relationships arise through language, and within particular socio-cultural environments, in response to human thinking about quantity, relationships, and space.

What we want to know now is how mathematical words come to mean just what they do? If other meanings were possible, or other mathematical structures could have existed, what was it that made mathematics as it is?

7.   METAPHORS

This section is about the origins of mathematics. It is necessary, therefore, that we take a look at a book with the title *Where Mathematics Comes From* (Lakoff & Núñez, 2000). Actually, first we need to see where the book itself comes from before we can use it to shed light on how a language might create a mathematical world.

Works by a group of cognitive linguists centred around George Lakoff have put forward a possible answer. They suggest that a set of metaphors develops in a language and becomes deeply embedded within that language. Furthermore some metaphors are more dominant than others in any one language. Lakoff has, for over twenty years, been writing about these metaphors (Lakoff & Johnson, 1980; Lakoff, 1987; Lakoff & Johnson, 1999; Lakoff & Núñez, 2000), and their use in deep and unconscious ways. The intriguingly entitled *Women, Fire, and Dangerous Things* is not a risky discourse on gender issues, but an analysis of how words are linked to meaning.

Lakoff looks at classical theories of meaning in which an object is linked to a word if it has the necessary characteristics. For example, the word *table* can be linked to a particular object if that object has all the *table* characteristics: flat surface, used for putting things on, legs to raise it off the floor, and so on. Thus the meaning of the word *table* is the set of table-characteristics. Lakoff then shows that this is not, actually, how we do ascribe meaning to a word. We do not simply look at an object and decide whether it has particular 'table' characteristics, and if it does then we call it a table. Meaning is a much more loose kind of reference, a network of connections. It is not true that objects are either tables or not-tables, depending on their characteristics. Some things can be more table-like than others, just as some things are more useful than others. Some things may be used as tables and referred to as tables temporarily when they are actually chairs or (heaven forbid) pianos. Some things may be described as a table by one person but not by another, although the characteristics of the object are not in question. Our conceptual categories are relational, blurred, and linked in chains of association. Lakoff talks about paradigms of tables, objects that epitomise the meaning of the word *table* and are used as reference points for less table-like objects.

An interesting parallel exists between the nature of categorisation that Lakoff has described in linguistic concepts, and a branch of set theory dealing with what are called Fuzzy Sets (Klir, St. Clair, & Bo Yuan, 1997). Fuzzy set theory allows 'partial' membership of sets: membership is described by a number between 0 (not a member) and 1 (a full member). If an object has a membership of 0.2, then it is a little bit a member of the set, if it has a membership of 0.9 then it is nearly completely a member. Similarly, Fuzzy logic allows things to be partially true. This branch of mathematics turns out to have very useful applications in the design of computer chips that are used in many household appliances like washing machines. Years after this theory was first developed, there are still many mathematicians who reject Fuzzy Set theory as not mathematics, or, if they admit it, then they regard it as insignificant mathematics. They do not seem to be able to step outside the conceptual boundary erected by classical categories. Lakoff has a theory that may explain such behaviour.

Now we come to the metaphors. Lakoff is interested in why Western linguists adopted classical theories of meaning when the theories do not describe how we actually use words? Where did this theory come from? His suggestion is that our thinking responds to very basic experiences that we have as human beings inhabiting our particular world. As he puts it, we have embodied minds, and our experiences provide us with the basic tools for thinking. Experiences like putting things in containers, travelling from one place to another, seeing things falling down to the ground, are so common and so fundamental in our world that they enter our minds as paradigms whether we are aware of it or not. He calls these metaphors, *grounding* metaphors for creating abstract thought, and *linking* metaphors for making connections between abstract conceptions. Note that these ideas of metaphors are not the same as the grammatical one. Grammatical metaphors refer to correspondences between experience and language, rather than correspondences in language between experiences.

For example, one grounding metaphor is the Container Metaphor. We put things in containers, they are either in or out. This is a fundamental and oft-repeated process in many, many contexts—and it has come to be a dominant metaphor in our thinking. Hence we have classical theories of meaning where meaning corresponds to putting things in a class (this object is a *table*, it is in the collection of objects to which we ascribe the word *table*) or leaving them out (this object is not a *table*). Lakoff suggests that the classical 'container' model of meaning is deeply embedded in English (and other Indo-European languages) so that we talk as if that is how categories are determined, when in fact they are not. Classical theorists have gone to considerable lengths to keep the model intact, discussing conditions for the application of characteristics of tables, or prioritising these characteristics, for example. The metaphor is extremely strong and we are loathe to give it up.

Another grounding metaphor is the Path Metaphor. We make journeys from one place to another, starting somewhere, moving along a path, and arriving somewhere else. An arrow does the same thing. This simple action sequence is repeated many times in human experience. Another of the insights Lakoff (and co-writer Johnson) makes (1999) is that different cultures, different philosophical traditions, different languages, privilege different metaphors. Thus the Container Metaphor is strong in Western thought, the Path Metaphor amongst the Hopi American First Nation people (Whorf, 1956). This idea can be used to explain why Navajo conceive of shapes as actions: their spatial concepts are dominated by the path metaphor, and the ways in which one might travel a path, rather than shapes as groups of things that can be put into sets (squares, circles, lines).

Let us keep thinking about mathematics. Lakoff does this, with Rafael Núñez, in *Where Mathematics Comes From* (Lakoff & Núñez, 2000). The idea of metaphors that guide our thinking is presented with strong evidence and solid argument. It is an attractive idea with strong explanatory potential. However, in the book about mathematics, Lakoff and Nùñez apply metaphors to every detail of our mathematical thinking, citing most aspects of mathematics from the addition process to grand conceptual insights as all being examples of base metaphors. In the words of a reviewer (Madden, 2001, p. 1185): "After a while, the notion of metaphor seems to become a catchall. ... [it] begins to lose its meaning." I like the metaphor idea to explain the broad orientations to mathematics, rather than its detail.

The same reviewer has two other criticisms of interest in our discussion about the origin of mathematics (Madden, 2001, p. 1184-6). One is that Lakoff and Núñez do not talk about how "metaphors function in the mathematical activities of actual people. ... How exactly do people use metaphors when they are learning new [mathematical] material, solving problems, proving theorems, and communicating with one another?" The other criticism is expressed as "If *my* mathematics depends on the metaphors that happen to be in my head, and *your* mathematics depends on the metaphors in yours, then how is it that we can share mathematical ideas? And why is it that we agree so much?"

A response to these questions lies in one of the conclusions reached from the evidence of language: mathematics emerges from communication. During communication people use natural language full of grounding metaphors based on common embodied experience. We have seen how, at least in everyday mathematical discourse, languages hold these grounding metaphors in their vocabulary, grammar, and discourse. As noted by Devlin, as the abstract mathematical ideas are communicated, discussed, argued, agreed upon, then this natural language facility is all that is needed, although it slowly develops from natural language into the particular structures and meanings of mathematical discourse—but the grounding metaphors remain throughout this process. Thus the metaphors enter mathematics through the communication that is a necessary part of mathematical creation, and we share mathematical ideas because they are developed through natural language into mathematical discourse. Now we can see why we agree so much: because natural language and mathematical language contain the same grounding metaphors.

The idea of grounding metaphors guiding the creation of abstract domains of thought can be clearly seen in mathematics. I chose to describe the Container metaphor and Path metaphor because they have a special place in the foundations of mathematics.

Lakoff's idea is that these metaphors are so embedded in the languages we speak that they become unconscious. Another way of describing this insight is to say that, whatever we are talking about, we are talking through metaphors. The Fields Medallist (mathematicians' equivalent of the Nobel Prize) Rene Thom has expressed the same idea (1992):

> I think it is, more or less, philosophically an illusion to distinguish between reality and metaphor. In fact, analogy is, to some extent, a deep phenomenon of our thinking and if we want to understand what analogy is, then we are led to very fundamental philosophical problems.

The Container metaphor is a deep part of Indo-European languages. What is the equivalent of the Container metaphor in mathematics? Set theory. A set is a mathematical structure represented by a collection of objects: they may be points (the collection of all points that are 2cm from a certain point will be a circle around that point), or numbers (for example the infinite set of even numbers), or even collections of things that you do, for example the collection of all the ways you can turn or reflect an equilateral triangle so that it remains looking the same. (You could rotate it about its centre by 120°, or 240°, or a complete turn; you could reflect it about any line through its centre and one of the corners. The collection of these six actions is a set).

Mathematicians use sets to build up mathematics. Starting from just the idea of a collection of objects, one can describe much of mathematics. During the early part of the 20th century, mathematicians gave themselves the task of setting mathematics on a firm foundation building it up from very basic ideas. And when it was achieved (or appeared to be achieved, it was later proved that the task was actually impossible), it was achieved with sets. Given that sets are the mathematical form of the Container metaphor, and that the foundations of mathematics were carried out mainly in Europe, it should be no surprise that set theory was the basic tool for describing these foundations.

Could it have been otherwise? What other foundations might there be? Certainly many mathematicians accept that there could be others, and that mathematics may never be completely understood in terms of any attempted foundations. Hermann Weyl has said (1944):

> The question of the ultimate foundations and the ultimate meaning of mathematics remains open: we do not know in what direction it will find its final solution or even whether a final objective answer can be expected at all. 'Mathematizing' may well be a creative activity of man, like language or music, of primary originality, whose historical decisions defy complete objective rationalisation.

One other foundation has been seriously attempted: the Category Theory of Saunders Mac Lane (1998), a theory which uses functions. Now functions are the equivalent of the Path metaphor in mathematics. The basic idea of a function is that you start with one object, and then transform it into another object. So, for example, start with a number, double it and add one, and you get another number. 2 goes to 5, 9 goes to 19, 103 goes to 207, and so on. This is written mathematically as:

$$f : x \rightarrow 2x + 1$$

Read as: "the function f takes x onto 2x + 1"

Usually, definitions of functions are made with reference to sets. However Mac Lane developed functions as the foundation of mathematics, that is, everything else is built up from the idea of functions: numbers, sets, geometric shapes, everything. Nor did he consider this to be the only alternative (1981, p. 469):

> The set-theoretic approach is by no means the only possible foundation for mathematics. Another approach is to formulate axioms on the composition of functions. This ... probably gives better insight into the conceptual form of mathematics than does set theory. There may well be other possible systematic foundations different from set-theoretic or categorical ones.

Let us combine the thoughts of Weyl and Mac Lane, with the grounding metaphors of Lakoff, and with our conclusions about mathematics and language. The strong suggestion emerges that if mathematics had developed through a language where the path metaphor was dominant, then the mathematics that would have emerged may have been dominated by functions, or some equivalent concept, rather than by sets. We have every reason to believe that this mathematics would have been just as powerful, and just as widely and effectively applicable: but it would have been different. The historical possibility of fundamentally different but equivalently sophisticated mathematics is the key conclusion of this book.

Remember the earlier analysis of Zeno's Arrow Paradox at the end of Chapter 2? The two contrasting formulations can now be interpreted as based on the Container and Path grounding metaphors respectively.

8.   MINDLOCKS

The language we speak affects the way we do mathematics, and the mathematics we do affects our language. There are two sides to this coin: a restricting one and an enabling one.

Mathematics is essentially a creative activity where anything seems possible, and where communication internationally between speakers of many languages reaches agreement on most fundamental questions. Thus many mathematicians reject the idea that they are, consciously or unconsciously, restricted or limited by anything, let alone the language they speak.

It is our experience that we can communicate the things that we think. Language enables us to communicate, it is endlessly creative, and it can adapt to new ideas. We sense that, if we did learn something new from someone who spoke a different language, then we would be able to express it more or less intact in our own language.

I believe this to be true—with some reservations. The first reservation is that I do not know whether I am *not* having some thoughts that I might otherwise have if I spoke another language. Second, my experience with other languages tells me that often there is something, some nuance, lost in the translation: ask anyone who speaks more than one language well whether there are ideas expressed in one language not fully translatable into another. And finally, some thoughts can be expressed in many ways, and I feel that the way that a thought does get expressed has an influence on where that thought is taken, how it is developed, or what other thoughts might follow on. What we have been discovering is that all of these reservations apply to mathematics. This "Queen of the Sciences" (a name attributed to Gauss) is not above such influences, nor does she rule them.

The pathways in our thinking shaped by the language we speak I call *mindlocks*. We are not normally aware of mindlocks because they are part of the very structure of our language and thought. It is possible to break out of them, but doing so requires an awareness that a mindlock is operating, and a conscious attempt to overcome it. Languages in general are rich enough, and flexible enough, to open mindlocks once they are identified: the problem is identifying them.

A good example of a mindlock is present in the above paragraph: "language and thought". In English we make a distinction between thought and language, but such a dichotomy may not always be a useful way of talking/thinking (Lee, 1996, pp. 72-79). Language and thought are so closely interconnected that making statements like: "thought comes before language" or "thought is dependent upon language" may not make much sense. Perhaps it would be better if we regarded them as different aspects of one human function. But how can I express this? Using the phrase "language and thought" preserves the distinction; using a term like "linguistic thinking" suggests that there can be non-linguistic thinking" (such as visual thinking); and a new compound word like "thanguage" or "langought" is likely to be so strange as to be disconcerting for a reader. However, having identified the mindlock, it is now possible to continue, being aware of this dichotomy that is preserved in English, but which is being called into question.

I do not intend to get into an argument here as to whether there is such a thing as visual thinking—the point is that such an argument is partly created by the way we separate language and thought in our speaking. The way English works encourages us to have such a question, on the one hand, but, on the other, English mitigates against consideration of the implications of thought and language being two sides of the same coin. This exemplifies the restricting and enabling function of mindlocks.

Mindlocks can be embedded in the vocabulary and in the categories that we use, as in the above example, or as a result of the grammar and syntax of the language, like the verbal numbers found in Polynesian languages. But the most difficult mindlocks to become aware of are those which are part of the ethos or world view presented by a language. Within mathematics, an example is the idea of rational argument or mathematical proof. The very word *rational* links this concept to the Greek origins of argument, the classical Trivium of Grammar, Rhetoric, and Logic. Asian or Indian forms of proof based on exemplification are not rational and thus tend to be excluded by English speakers as not being sensible or reasonable since that is what the word *rational* has come to mean.

Maps present a good example of an embedded world view. The predominant north/south orientation of maps has come to be fixed in our language. We go "up north" and "down south", and "over to the west or east". In Milton Keynes in England all the main north-south roads are labelled V (for vertical) and the east-west ones are H (for horizontal). We hold maps with north upwards on the page, or ahead of us if flat. The tourist map of New Zealand that shows the world with south at the top, (and hence New Zealand on top of the world instead of at the bottom) is described as upside down. We look at maps with north ahead of us even if we are ourselves facing south. We might travel down (south) to a ski-field from a more northerly location although, being in the mountains, it is considerably higher (more elevated). These ways of talking reinforce the assertion that orientation is only a convention. Our conventional orientation is rarely questioned, although it is far from universal. In the old Arab world maps were conventionally drawn with south at the top of the page (Bagrow, 1985, pp. 57-58). In New Zealand, the Maori vision of the North Island is a fish with its tail at the north end, and mouth at Wellington: hence, in Maori, *"Haere ki runga a Te Upoko o Te Ika"*, or "Go up to the head of the fish", means to travel southwards.

Is everything we say a mindlock? Well, it could be. Every part of our language contributes to those mindlocks that infuse the language. Our vocabulary, our grammar, our syntax, our discourse, our grounding metaphors. However such thinking can make the whole discussion very negative and limiting. We have to use some kind of language, so it is just as sensible to say that language enables us to think or to communicate any thoughts at all, as it is to say that language restricts us from thinking in certain ways. When I first thought of the word *mindlock*, I was thinking about locks in canals: those narrow channels that help control rivers and that provide means for boats to reach higher levels. These locks represent a means for higher thinking, but they are also fixed in one place and control the flow of traffic.

At the end of Part I we discussed the idea of mathematical world views. These can be regarded as a system of mindlocks. Languages that are different from Indo-European ones have been examined for the ways they express ideas of quantity, space, and relationships. We have identified some structures and patterns that differ from the structures and patterns of the Indo-European languages. The latter, however, have been developed into the academic field we know as mathematics. I draw the conclusion that mathematics might have been otherwise, that it could have been caught up in a different set of mindlocks.

In the next section the development of mathematics, rather than its origins, is discussed. Again the role of language mindlocks will emerge, and a couple of worrying consequences of the link between mathematics and language will be discussed.

Chapter 6

A NEVER-ENDING BRAID:
THE DEVELOPMENT OF MATHEMATICS

Abstract: The evidence from language is brought together to discuss the nature of mathematics. Different conceptions of the way it develops are described, and the mechanisms that operate in its development are hypothesised. The Kama Sutra is invoked to illustrate the links between mathematics and society.

Keywords: philosophy of mathematics, history of mathematics, nature of mathematics

Douglas Hofstadter (1979) referred to mathematical thought as *The Eternal Golden Braid*. This book wove together mathematics in the form of the work of Kurt Gödel, graphic art as drawn by M. C. Escher, and music as epitomised in the Bach symphonies. The dominant theme of self-reference was played out through each of these human creations in such a way that the works that I knew (the mathematics and the graphic art) enlightened me on the work that I did not really understand (Bach's music). I had the feeling that it would be possible for any reader who knew well any two of the fields, to similarly reach an appreciation of the third.

Three different worlds dealt with the same theme differently but in depth, creating an image of a braid with the three strands weaving together and gaining strength from the existence of each other. They could never be the same, nor could one of them ever be encompassed by any other. Each creation had its own aspects that could not be adequately represented in the other: the abstract austerity of Gödel's mathematics, the emotional intensity of Bach's music, the aesthetic playfulness of Escher's etchings.

Hofstadter did not suggest the three pieces of work had the same origin, nor could I conceive how they might ever be completely amalgamated by some wider, more general activity. It reminded me of Hermann Hess' (2002) book *The Glass Bead Game*, and the imaginary "performance" of the maestro as he wove together literature, language, music, mathematics, art, dance, and other forms of cultural expression in a symphony of words, a picture of equations, and a poem of forms.

The idea of human creativity bringing together different forms in ever new combinations is a model that could be adopted for mathematics itself. Such a model is quite different from the commonly accepted idea that mathematics is one ever expanding stream, fed by tributaries that get encompassed by the main current in broader generalisation, higher levels of abstraction, or reorganisation of the components of mathematics.

But isn't it true that the mathematical stream is fed by its tributaries? When the mathematical community becomes aware of a new idea, it is accommodated into mathematics for the benefit of all. For example, when a mathematician became interested in the *kolam* patterns drawn by Indian women on their doorsteps (Ascher, 2002), and realised that the system represented there was not only mathematical but also contained some new mathematical ideas, he did not turn away from mathematics and work with the women to develop *kolam* further. He reinterpreted what he had seen using mathematical notation and wrote about it in a mathematical journal of an appropriate existing mathematical field (Siromoney, 1986; Siromoney & Sironmoney, 1987). In this case it was the mathematical aspects of computer science. The scientist was interested in the structure of "languages" used to describe drawings. He had worked with strings of symbols and how they could be used as a "language" for pictures. Watching women making *kolam* patterns he realised that another method for developing a language could be to create an array of symbols, as the women built an array first, before drawing their patterns. This was a new mathematical idea generated by the traditional craft.

Put another way, if there are other mathematical worlds as indicated by the evidence from language, why have they not been developed? Where are these other mathematical worlds? Could it be the case that mathematics as we know it is, in fact, universal; that it can express every abstract structure or system in our world? Perhaps the absence of other mathematical worlds implies that nothing useful could come of them that cannot be done equally well in mathematics as we know it?

I want to use the image of a braid to try to answer some of these questions, so let us look at another example to get a feel for this mathematical braid.

1. PACIFIC NAVIGATION: IS IT MATHEMATICS?

In Part I there is a short description of the navigation techniques of Pacific navigators, the way they used paths rather than positions, and the orientation system called *etak*. Another technique used by skilled navigators was the analysis of swells in the ocean.

One of the features of the mid-Pacific is that it is a relatively predictable environment. While there are storms and weather changes, many of these are seasonal, and most of the weather is fine. Thus the trade winds are both steady in force and direction, and navigators can use them for orientation. Similarly, the reliable fine weather means that clouds form over islands, and can be seen from a distance when the land is over the horizon, making a much bigger "target" for a navigator to aim at. These constant environmental features are also reflected in the ocean swells. Even swells caused by storms are constant over several days.

The reliability of ocean swells can be useful information for a sea-farer. Swells are affected by the presence of islands, since swells change direction as they pass by. Surfers know this, the effect of land on swell direction is why good surfing is to be found off promontories: the swell bends as it rounds the promontory, creating a wave on which the break starts at one end and then runs along the length of the wave.

Thus the swells under your boat carry a lot of information if only you can read it: information about islands that are over the horizon; information about weather patterns; information about wind direction and strength. Pacific navigators used this information in quite systematic ways. The ancient navigation schools created models out of sticks and shells to teach their new navigators about swells, and every navigator learned what swells they could expect in different seasons, and how the swells would change, as they traversed each journey in their repertoire.

However, the first problem is to be able to detect the swells. It is reported (Gladwin, 1970, p. 170–4; Kyselka, 1987; Lewis, 1975, p. 90–3; Thomas, 1987) that Pacific navigators could feel the swells coming from four different directions simultaneously—the most famous contemporary navigator Mau could detect five (Kyselka, 1987, p. 98). That is, the navigators could feel the way the boat moved (even from inside the cabin at night) and thereby distinguish the movement of swells coming from several directions at the same time. The problem of discriminating component waves from the total wave movement is easily describable using the language of mathematics, and is a familiar problem when the waves are all from the same direction—this is the field known as Fourier or Harmonic Analysis. There has been little work done on the problem of multi-directional wave analysis, but mathematicians have no difficulty discussing it and accepting it as a problem in mathematics. They can generalise from the one-dimensional problem to that of waves coming from several directions, concept-ualising the difficulties of analysis, and identifying possible ways to get the solutions. The problem of two waves coming at right angles to each other can be solved computationally, using computers to get approxi-mations. But the problem has not been solved for waves coming from four different directions, and no instruments have been developed that will quickly resolve a wave movement into four directional com-ponents.

Now let us imagine again. Think of all the mathematical and technological effort that went into the development of navigation: star, moon and sun position charts; sighting equipment; the accurate timepieces needed to make use of these sightings to determine latitude and longitude; and modern GPS (Global Positioning System) equip-ment. Imagine that all (even a good fraction of) that money and effort had been put into analysis of wave motion and developing technology to sense swells in the ocean. Perhaps, if this had happened, ships would now be equipped with such sensors, and would have computer systems that could resolve the information and detect changes in the size and directions of the swells under their hulls.

If such things had been developed, then captains would have another piece of navigation equipment—a piece that would be able to warn them of small islands, or icebergs, in their vicinity before they became visible to lookouts or radar. And if the Titanic had had such a piece of technology, then alarm bells might have been automatically triggered all over the ship well before she ripped her bottom out with such tragic results on an iceberg no-one had seen. Perhaps the lawyers of Star Line should start looking for who was responsible for shaping the course of mathematical development?

This story of unrealised mathematical development, however far-fetched, illustrates what might have happened if mathematicians had become interested in the systems of Pacific navigators. We can imagine that harmonic analysis would be much further advanced than it is. This is what happens. Mathematics absorbs good ideas, techniques, even symbol systems, and makes them part of the mainstream of the subject. The worth of the ideas are judged on mathematical grounds. But this is not a braid with independent strands woven together but retaining their individuality, this is a river with tributaries flowing in. However, we can reverse the situation.

There is another story, a real story, about Pacific navigation. In Hawaii there is a Polynesian Voyaging Society (<http://pvs.kcc.hawaii.edu/welcome.html>) that was established in 1973. There is another one in Tahiti. Many countries have established schools and courses in these navigation techniques. Ocean-going canoes are being built, both authentic replicas and modern versions, and are being sailed across the Pacific to take part in national celebrations, competitions, cultural exchanges, and on research voyages. Thor Heyerdahl's re-creation of a voyage from South America was the first that became well-known (Heyerdahl, 1958)—is it because he was a European, or is it just because he knew how to manipulate the media?

In these schools, on these boats, and as part of the curriculum for these courses, there is often mention of modern navigation techniques, use of modern equipment, and training in mathematical ideas. However these are used to enhance the development and activity of navigation derived from the original techniques. Ideas are co-opted, techniques are absorbed, mathematical systems are adapted to the necessities of Pacific navigation, and are judged useful or not according to its criteria. If this sounds like what is written two paragraphs back from the point of view of mathematics, then good. The parallel is exact.

It may be argued that what happens in Pacific navigation schools is not mathematics, it is navigation. Navigation uses mathematics, just like many applied sciences. A picture of a braid woven together with independent strands of its applications is easy to accept. If a collection of applied mathematics strands is all that is meant by the braid, then the history of mainstream mathematical development is not challenged. But the braid being argued for here is a braid of mathematical strands.

Remember, in the introduction, the difficulty with the word 'mathematics' was noted. Every time this word is used it conjures up connotations, based on personal experience, of school mathematics, university mathematics, mathematics as we know it now. We have been calling this NUC-mathematics. When producing an argument that involves a broadening of the concept of mathematics, there is a problem with how to express it. We need to escape the mindlock.

Let us return to the widened idea of mathematics, that of a QRS-system—a system developed to give meaning to the quantitative, relational, or spatial aspects of our world. Let us put some further requirements on a QRS-system, requirements that are usually associated with NUC-mathematics: reproducibility, levels of abstraction, generalisability, and symbolisation. Now look again at Pacific navigation.

David Turnbull (1991, p. 23), when considering Micronesian navigation, asks the question: "What is a navigation system"? Some characteristics mentioned are: it should be symbolic (and therefore transmittable); it should be manipulable (and therefore adaptable); it should be generalised (and therefore non-localised); and it should be open (and therefore innovating). Gladwin (1970) describes the system of navigation on Puluwat atoll. His (and others') descriptions were further analysed by Hutchins (1983) in a way that made it clear that Turnbull's characteristics are met. To quote Hutchins (1993, p. 223) "The Micronesian technique is elegant and effective. It is organised in a way that allows the navigator to solve in his head, problems that a Western navigator would not attempt without substantial technological support".

Pacific navigation is not mathematics. Pacific navigation is not itself a QRS-system. But Pacific navigation does contain a QRS-system. Pacific navigation contains its own mathematics, a mathematics that is different in some fundamental ways from NUC-mathematics. For example, its criteria of accuracy are different (path accuracy is different from positional accuracy or distance), and its abstractions are different (path form is more important than map scale, and any scales may be time-based rather than length-based). We can discuss one set of criteria in terms of the other. We can transform the maps from one system to the other. That does not make them the same thing, nor can we assume that all features of the system are transformed intact.

The strand in the mathematical braid that carries the Pacific navigation QRS-system is smaller than that of NUC-mathematics. It is also wrapped inside a 'Pacific navigation' covering, but it is a mathematical braid nevertheless. The mathematics of standard, positional navigation remains as a fibre in the mainstream mathematical strand.

The picture of our mathematical braid is now one of a thick strand of NUC-mathematics woven with many smaller, braids that are disguised with other names. We have found a way of distinguishing different mathematics, no matter how limited in their application. Now let us look again at the main strand of NUC-mathematics. Is it what it seems?

2.   A RIVER OR A BRAID?

When travelling to countries where you speak only a little of the language, or when talking to visitors who only speak a little of your language, a common response is to restrict the conversation to those things that are easily discussed, but about which there is likely to be common interest and agreement. As new grandparents spending six months in Spain, my wife and I became very competent at asking others, in Spanish, about their families: brothers and sisters, parents, children. If we were lucky and the people we met also had grandchildren, then we could hold a conversation that made us feel we could really speak Spanish, instead of the reality that we just had a minor facility in a couple of restricted areas. Always such conversations felt good, and left us smiling, and it wasn't just the remembered antics of Zephyr and Veronica. It was the joy of communication and shared common feeling.

Mathematics is a bit like this. That is to say, one of the mechanisms of mathematics is to focus on common features. It is natural that, when mathematicians talk, there is a tendency to talk about ideas that they have in common—we all do this, in every conversation. Even arguments depend on agreement on the topic and usually on the means of persuasion, although it does not always seem like it.

Some arguments do result from people talking past each other. These arguments are often unresolved, and usually lead to a feeling of dissatisfaction. Talking past each other can be cultural in origin.

My introduction to the phrase was in the title of a book for teachers (Metge, 1978) about cultural protocols and the misunderstandings they produce in classroom interactions. The result is alienation and isolation.

Since mathematics is formed and developed through communication, a consequence is that those parts of mathematics that get developed are those about which there is agreement. The areas of disagreement get dropped, or are only developed with difficulty. When research mathematicians come together in international communities, there are inevitably some difficulties of communication. Agreed symbolisms and definitions of mathematics make communication easier—but within a restricted domain. Here is the key point: that domain is restricted by the very agreements that make the communication possible. Where a definition is not agreed, or the nature of a named concept is different for different mathematicians, then we encounter talking past each other. Three examples of this have already been mentioned: non-standard analysis, the mathematics developed from Cauchy's concept of the continuum; the divergent paths of statistical analysis deriving from the two conceptions of probability; and Category Theory, the foundations of mathematics being written using functions, not sets.

What happens, however, is that these differences are, in some way, made invisible. There are several reasons for this, and several ways that it can happen. But the end result is the preservation of the sense that all mathematics is proceeding together in one large stream, a stream of different interests, but one stream nevertheless, with the happy family of mathematicians floating together along it. This may be what mathematicians feel, but below the surface, mathematics is made up of quite different ideas being developed, often interacting, and knowing of each other's existence, but conceptually different in important ways. Hence, the metaphor of a braid of many strands and fibres, is more appropriate than that of a river with tributaries.

One more important issue. The researchers in the international community of mathematicians are increasingly using only one language to communicate: English. It was noted above that mathematical communication is restricted by the agreements that make communication possible. One of those agreements is to use English. So mathematics is becoming increasingly restricted to the ideas that can be expressed in English, and mathematical development will increasingly be directed down paths that are privileged by English. This is not a new idea.

In the first half of last century, the linguist Benjamin Whorf wrote (1956, p. 244):

> ... but to restrict thinking to the patterns merely of English, and especially to those patterns which represent the acme of plainness in English, is to lose a power of thought which, once lost, can never be regained. It is the "plainest" English which contains the greatest number of unconscious assumptions about nature. ... Western culture has made, through language, a provisional analysis of reality and, without correctives, holds resolutely to that analysis as final.

If we have a thought or understand a concept, it can be expressed in English or any other language. All languages are endlessly creative and adaptable, and once aware of mis-communication or nuances in ideas that are not expressed in a particular language, then it is possible to find a way to express what was missed. The point is that there are some thoughts that are unlikely to occur at all if only one language is used.

Perhaps this is more clearly seen in another development, the communication of mathematics over the web. There are many mathematical systems on the web: Matlab, Maple, Mathematica, for example. Mathematicians routinely use these systems to generate and explore hypotheses, to test ideas, and to communicate with each other. A recent development is the building of a mathematical language from very basic concepts, basic enough that all the different mathematical systems can be written using these concepts (Borwein, 1999). Once that has been achieved, all the systems can be linked together, and can communicate with each other. This basic language is intended to become *the* language of mathematics. Given what we have said, the danger is apparent. Only mathematical ideas that can be expressed in this language are likely to be developed—or, at the very least, mathematical ideas expressable in this language will be strongly privileged. Do the writers of the mathematical web language really believe that they can write a universal language that will accommodate all future mathematical ideas?

In the mathematics braid some strands are bigger than others, some strands merge with each other or split apart, some strands are disguised within non-mathematical coverings. But if we regard mathematics as QRS-systems, I argue that mathematics consists of parallel systems, not one consistent body. Ethnomathematics can be regarded as the study of the different fibres of mathematical knowledge.

Such an image calls into question the universal origin of mathematics. There is no reason to assume that, at the beginning of the braid, there was only one strand. Indeed, if we look at the current situation where there is a tendency towards convergence of ideas, the more likely scenario is that mathematics had multiple origins. Joseph's diagrams (1992, Figs. 1.1–1.4) of the very early development of mathematics expose the paucity of what he calls a Eurocentric model of the history of mathematics. His final picture details the plaiting of the mathematical braid in the early millennia of mathematical thought. An argument of this book is that increased communication amongst mathematicians leads not to a single stream, but to more complex plaiting of many braids.

I believe that it is important, for mathematics, for human development, and for mathematics education, that we start to focus on differences between strands as much as points of similarity. If mathematics is to continue to blossom, and to express all the things that human thought can achieve, then we must resist any convergence of what is investigated. To do that we need to understand more about how the restrictions occur. That is the next topic.

3.   SNAPPING TO GRID AND OTHER MECHANISMS

Take a trip, if you will, to Hawai'i, renowned for its tourist hotels, beaches, pineapples, and big surf. Hawai'i was—still is—a centre of traditional Pacific navigation and sea-faring. Of course, for a sea-farer, winds are critical, and the trade winds, being so constant, are a good source of information and direction. Thus words associated with winds are going to be important. One such word is the word for *leeward*. In Hawaiian this is *lalo*. Given the north-east trade winds, this would be used for the south-eastern side of the islands.

Now, Hawaiian is a Polynesian language, and there are some simple transformations that generally apply to this family of languages when you move from one to the other. To move from Hawaiian to Maori, the 'l' becomes a 'r'. Thus *lalo* becomes *raro*. In Maori, *raro* means 'under' or 'north', particularly when associated with the wind. I cannot find any Maori word for *leeward*. Is there a relationship between the Hawaiian *lalo* (leeward) and the Maori word *raro* (north)?

In New Zealand, could the word *raro* have originally meant *leeward*? New Zealand is far enough into the southerly ocean that the dominant wind is the cold southerly or south-westerly. Thus leeward would be in the north or north-east. Or, perhaps, *raro* just had the other meaning of *under*. As noted before, the North Island of New Zealand is *Te Ika a Maui* (The Fish of Maui) and its head is at the bottom where Wellington now sits. That is why this region is known as *Te Upoko o te Ika*—The Head of the Fish. When you travel to the tail of the fish, that is the north-northwest part of the country, you go down. Under. *Raro*.

Whichever of these explanations is correct, *raro* meant either north-northeast or north-northwest, but referred to important characteristics of the geography of the country, not to due north.

When the Europeans arrived with their NSEW compass as a dominant reference, it seems likely that the word for the direction closest to north got adapted to due north. At this point one reference system transfers to another, and the language changes in response to a shift in spatial system. In contemporary dictionaries, *raro* means north. The phrase "snap-to-grid" is familiar to those who have tried to draw pictures in their Word documents on a computer. The lines automatically adjust to an invisible grid on the page, moving slightly from where you place them so that they join up exactly.

I wonder if the early attempts to create Maori word-lists also contain an example of this effect. Trinick (1999) reports that:

> In 1793, Lieutenant-Governor King of New South Wales, Australia visited the northern part of the North Island [of New Zealand] and collected information relating to the country and Maori. The information collected was published in Collin's *History of New South Wales* in 1804. The Maori numerals (pp 562) are misspelt but recognisable;
>
> 1: Ta-hie *(Tahi)*   2: **Du-o** *(Rua)*   3: Too-roo*(Toru)*   ....

The accepted Maori words are in brackets. It is curious that the only sound that is clearly wrong is the 'o' on 'duo' (the Maori 'r' sound is very like a 'd'). Could this be an unconscious slip because Italian (and Latin, which, presumably the educated Governor would have known) have the word 'duo' for two?

"Snapping-to-grid" is one of the Universalising mechanisms by which mathematical development hides its differences or unifies itself.

Universalising mechanisms is the name I give to the ways in which mathematics normalises or links new ideas to the conventional mainstream, whatever their origins, (for further discussion see Barton, 1996, Section 4.3). If unification is successfully achieved, then there is no challenge to the rationality or correctness of existing mathematics. Rather, it enhances the subject by showing it to be, yet again, robust enough to accommodate new ideas, or even more richly intertwined.

During this process radical change may occur. Mathematical terms and concepts are continuously created, or may be re-created in the form of the old, but with new substance. Thus there is the appearance of old terms encompassing the new situations, when, in fact, new concepts are involved.

"Snapping-to-Grid" is a Universalising mechanism that is like colonisation. It transforms new ideas into existing terminology, thereby stripping them of their distinctive aspects, and, in particular, removing cultural characteristics. The ideas are acknowledged to be mathematics, but are not acknowledged to be mathematically new. The most common example is the way counting terminology in different cultures is transformed into direct equivalents of one, two, three, four, ... in the cardinal mathematical sense. The words may never have been used in this sense, as an example in addition to those in Chapter 3, in Burmese, the vast array of number classifiers (Burling, 1965) for use in different situations reduce to a single set for mathematical discourse.

The justification for such colonising is the principle that stripping of context is exactly what mathematics is about. Practices from other cultures are interesting only in so far as the 'real' mathematics can be found. What is forgotten in this justification is that mathematics has a context expressed through the language and symbolic conventions of its host culture. An effect of implying that any new ideas are merely reformulations of ideas already part of mathematics, is to maintain the source of the new ideas in an inferior position. Thus cultures that do not have counting words beyond 50, say, are demonstrated to be less mathematically sophisticated. Such notions lead to the idea of primitive cultures (Stigler & Baranes, 1988).

Another Universalising mechanism is subsumption. Subsuming mathematical ideas does not involve translation of the idea into new terminology, it relegates the idea to the status of an example. Like colonisation, the implication is that the idea is not new; unlike colonisation, the idea is not even regarded as mathematics itself, just as an example. Such examples are welcomed as interesting, and educationally illustrative, but they are not worthwhile in a mathematical sense. This is 'artefact' mathematics. An example of this mechanism is the identification of certain types of artistic decoration as mathematical. For example, in New Zealand, the Maori *kowhaiwhai* (rafter patterns from Maori Meeting houses) are recognised as mathematical strip patterns exhibiting symmetric groups and used in school publications to teach transformation geometry.

The result of this process does not necessarily remove the mathematical idea from its cultural context. On the contrary, the retention of its cultural surroundings is exactly what is required when subsumption occurs in an educational context. But the effect is to reinforce the idea that a cultural context can only be an example of mathematics, it is not mathematics itself. Any different, deep mathematical idea behind the artefact is now even less likely to be examined.

Yet complex ideas in mathematics can be found in cultural craft practices. The patterns formed in the weaving of Maori flax baskets (Pendergast, 1984, 1987) were also used to demonstrate mathematical groups and used in school resources (Knight, 1985). In doing this the conventional NUC-mathematics criteria of symmetry were used for classification. But the Maori names for these patterns form a different classification, grouping together patterns that are not easily recognised as similar in our eyes. However, to a weaver's eyes, the groups make sense: the classification depends on how the initial strands are set up. One group comes from strands set up as alternating white, black, white, black, white, black, white, and then different patterns made by different weaving; in another group the strands are white, white, black, white, black, white, black, white, black, white, white, ... (see Fig 6-1).

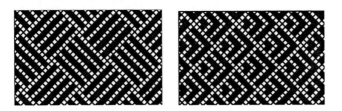

Figure 6-1. Weaving patterns from the same strand set-up

The two classification systems are not compatible, but are equally mathematical. I once used the 'strand set-up' classification as a talk on triple weaving patterns to a group of mathematicians, and discussed how two-colour patterns could transform into each other. The response? "Ah," said a colleague, "your transformation group looks like a structure from hyperbolic geometry".

The justification for subsumption is the principle that mathematics provides powerful ideas for solving a variety of situations. Therefore the identification of a known idea in a new situation, provides another opportunity to apply known results. Sociologically, subsumption has the effect of establishing status. If one idea is accepted as an example of another, then the example is relegated to a lower status, and its originating context is deprived of the intellectual credit.

A third Universalising mechanism I call appropriation. Appropriation of new ideas acknowledges the novelty in the ideas (unlike snapping-to-grid or subsumption), but assumes that they form part of an existing mathematical structure. This is done either by regarding the new idea as a new category in an existing hierarchy, or by creating a new generalisation under which existing mathematics and the new idea will both fit. In this process the mathematical concepts may change, for example 'logic' now includes multi-value logic although it originally only referred to Aristotelian logic. The appropriation effect becomes clear: it is assumed that Aristotelian logic provided the foundation for today's logic, when it only provided the etymological origins. The investigation of swells as advanced Fourier Analysis could be another example of this.

The justification for appropriation is the assumption of generalisability: it is always possible to obtain a mathematical idea of greater generality to bring together previously unrelated concepts. Generalising usually involves greater abstraction, and the mechanism provides a way to reapply existing knowledge to new situations. The danger with this process is that once a generalisation has been made it is more difficult to perform a different generalisation. The assumption of universal structure mitigates against seeking other abstractions once the idea has been fitted into one satisfactory hierarchy. The sensation of a single universal structure is thereby enhanced.

4.   REJECTION AND ISOLATION

The three Universalising mechanisms in which mathematics draws in ideas from other areas are complemented by ways in which it can reject other ideas if they do not fit with existing mathematical conventions by labelling them as something other than mathematics. I call processes of rejection Isolating mechanisms. The effect is to retain mathematics as a stable and 'true' field, not allowing other forms of 'truth' to be called mathematics. This can be successfully achieved because the arbiters of mathematics are mathematicians themselves. Society in general cannot tell mathematicians what their field is like.

The first Isolating mechanism is non-recognition, or the rejection of the idea as having anything to do with 'proper' mathematics. The people who have the power to define mathematics, for example, journal editors, appointment committees, or curriculum designers, place the new idea outside the borders of the field.

An example is the attitude of many mathematicians towards much of the mathematics originating in the East. Joseph (1992) and Berrgren (1990) have both documented the rejection of much of the mathematics from India, China, and medieval Islam as non-rigorous. The results are only accepted after they have been proven in an acceptable (Western) manner. When they are proven, or analysed, they carry the name of the Western mathematician who did the work: hence we have Pascal's Triangle and Pythagoras' Theorem when these ideas were known for centuries before Pascal and Pythagoras. Knowledge of Pascal's Triangle is attributed to Jia Xian who lived 600 years before Pascal (Stillwell, 1989, p. 136). Evidence of Pythagoras' Theorem can be found in the Chinese text *Chou Pei Suang Ching* that may date from 500 years before Pythagoras (Swetz & Kao, 1977, p. 14). One of the subtleties of this mechanism is the way that the number of new theorems is taken as the measure of mathematics achievement (Davis & Hersh, 1981, pp. 20–25). People who do not (or did not) prove theorems are therefore not mathematicians.

The justification for non-recognition is the importance of convention as a basis for mathematical knowledge. How can mathematicians be sure of their results if there is a variety of foundations for the acceptance of mathematics? Sociologically, it is only by establishing the boundaries of a discipline that those within it can control their own activities. However, making the contrary statement: "this IS mathematics", and exploring the possibilities which are thereby opened up can be interesting. For example, Marcia Ascher explores the set theoretic structure of inheritance patterns (Ascher, 1991, pp. 72–76), and investigates the mathematical ideas that could newly illuminate a game analysis, such as the Maori game Mu Torere (Ascher, 1991, pp. 97–108).

Dismissal is a second Isolating mechanism. It recognises the mathematical component of a new idea but makes it unworthy of consideration. The new idea may not be described in acceptable terms, in an appropriate forum, or by someone of the required status. The effect is to devalue the new idea. The justification for dismissal is the maintenance of standards, but sociologically it can be seen as legitimisation. Social systems regulate themselves in various ways, from formal regulations to sub-conscious peer-pressure.

A famous example is the rejection of Ramanujan's manuscripts (Hardy, 1978, Preface). These contained some of the best mathematics of the century, but had been previously rejected without comment by two notable English mathematicians of the time to whom they had been sent before Hardy recognised their worth.

Another Isolating mechanism is compartmentalisation. It recognises the mathematical nature of the new idea, but places it outside mathematics proper, into a related discipline or a new field. This mechanism often carries inferior connotations, for example the 'number crunching' label attached to numerical analysis (the mathem-atics of computer methods) in its early years. Mathematical computing is a good example of an area which has established itself sufficiently to now affect the nature of mathematics itself (Epstein & Levy, 1995).

A historical example is the work of Florence Nightingale. No-one has ever recognised as a mathematical achievement her analysis of the causes of high mortality in field hospitals and maternity wards. It is now acknowledged to be a forerunner to the development of statistics as a discipline (Cohen, 1984), but at that time, such a field did not exist. Locating it now as statistics is partly to deny her work as mathematics.

Universalising and Isolating mechanisms not only occur as part of the colonial process when mathematical ideas from two cultures meet—as when Western reference systems dominated Pacific ones— but also operate internally within mathematics.

A request to a group of my mathematical colleagues to give me examples of Universalising resulted in each of them thinking of personal experiences where one thing they were working on or thinking about was suddenly "snapped to grid" or subsumed by another existing mathematical idea. The results are not always negative. The most famous example is Vaughan Jones' discovery of his knot invariants (now called the Jones polynomial). In the words of my colleague (Conder, Personal communication, 2006):

> He was working on aspects of subfactors of von Neumann algebras, and derived some equations associated with these, that turned out to look just like the braid relations from knot theory. Joan Birman and others helped him to "snap to the grid" of knot theory, and the rest is ... well ... history! This happens all the time, but usually not so spectacularly! [The 'history' in this case, was the Fields Medal, the mathematical equivalent of a Nobel Prize].

Lakatos (1976) talks about "monster-barring" as the way that mathematicians defend their proofs against counter-examples. This can be interpreted as a form of the Isolating mechanism non-recognition: the mathematician does not recognise the counter-example as relevant to the particular class of objects under discussion.

What has just been described are several ways in which the discipline of mathematics preserves the idea that it is a universal subject based on a single set of principles. This description is necessary if the argument of this book is to be accepted: if mathematics is to be seen as a braid of many strands, then it is necessary to explain why it has seemed like a river fed by tributaries.

I am not making a negative value-judgement, nor suggesting that mathematicians must start behaving differently. Rather, it is an attempt at a description of what happens. We need to recognise these processes if we are to fully understand the nature of our subject. Understanding what happens enables us to take another look at our field, to ask some other questions, and thereby consider other approaches to mathematical ideas that may be productive.

5. MATHEMATICS, SOCIETY & CULTURE

My Universalising and Isolating mechanisms are not the first attempt to describe what is happening in mathematics that explains its apparent universality. Others have written sociological accounts of mathematical knowledge, from Spengler, to Bloor, to Restivo (E.g. Spengler, 1926; Bloor, 1973, 1976, 1994; Restivo, 1983, 1992, 1993). Bloor, in particular, has attempted to use the anthropological theories of Mary Douglas to describe the Lakatos version of mathematical development (Bloor, 1978).

His programme has an even stronger aim than this. He seeks to break down the reification of mathematics as beyond sociological explanation (Bloor, 1973, p. 190), and to describe the mechanisms by which social and institutional circumstances (I would want to add cultural context) strongly determine the knowledge that scientists produce.

He focuses on mathematics and logic because this form of knowledge has been regarded as the most rational, a priori, and therefore the least likely to have sociological foundations. Bloor presents a number of examples of existing alternative forms of mathematical thought, and speculates on their social causes. For example (Bloor, 1976, pp. 125–9), he argues that the crises surrounding the development of calculus and the use of infinitesimals arose solely because the mathematicians attitudes to rigour had changed. The decline in rigour in the sixteenth century, in recognition of the practical results non-rigorous methods produced, actually allowed the infinitesimals to appear in calculations for the first time. The renewed interest in rigour in the nineteenth century produced a crises where there was not one before—and out of that crisis arose new mathematics.

Bloor also examines the historical process for the way in which it covers up variation, and concludes that the cumulative nature of mathematical development needs to be challenged. In responding to critics of his view (1976, pp. 179–83), he again makes the point that marginalisation of alternative mathematics' does not negate them, it just shows how a social cause creates an illusion of absolute knowledge.

Bloor's later work on mathematics (1983, Chpt. 5.; 1994) draws heavily on a Wittgensteinian analysis of the nature of mathematics to justify the idea that we construct conventions of meanings about numbers and relations as much as about words. The sociology of mathematics, in his view, aims to expose those conventions which have operated.

Davis (Davis, 1993, pp. 189ff) has also written about the relationship between mathematics and society. He argues that mathematics constitutes a way of thinking which is different from other ways, and that different ways of thinking need to be balanced in our society. For example, there has been a long literature concerning the use of mathematics in the social sciences. Kaplan (1960) gives an account of some early attempts—including a mathematical characterisation of sociology itself in which every social situation may be described by an equation. Catastrophe Theory, developments in Game Theory, and mathematical theories of politics all contribute to the mathematisation of social science. But it is not just the encroachment of mathematics into social life which is the subject of Davis' concern. He argues that computerisation, for example, has fundamentally changed our modes of thinking (Davis & Hersh, 1986).

For Davis, the balance of mathematical versus other types of thinking is to be achieved through education, hence (Davis, 1993, p. 190):

> I should like to argue that mathematics instruction should, over the next generation, be *radically* changed. It should be moved up from subject-oriented instruction to instruction in what the mathematical structures and processes mean in their own terms and what they mean when they form a basis on which civilization conducts its own affairs. .... [This requires] the teacher to become an interpreter and a critic of the mathematical processes and of the way these processes interact with knowledge as a database.

He sums up:

> If mathematics is a language, it is time to put an end to overconcentration on its grammar and to study the "literature" that mathematics has created and to interpret that literature.

Davis' makes a convincing case for this consequence of a sociological view of mathematics. The case is even more persuasive if a world view description of mathematics is correct. If there are alternative mathematical languages which may be encultured in any education system, it is imperative that every society produces the means to question these ways of thought, and to make informed choices about how dominant they are to become. This theme is developed further in the next section.

But finally, to finish this chapter, and before we turn to the philosophical implications of these ideas, let us take a small diversion into the world of the Kama Sutra and discuss the issue of mathematics in society.

We are familiar with the uses of mathematics in science, technology, economics, and industry. Mathematics as an applied science seems to provide the *raison d'etre* for the investment and effort that societies spend on mathematical development. Yet many mathematicians claim that the real reason for studying the subject is its own joys (Hardy, 1941), and David Singmaster's Chronology of Recreational Mathematics (2006) goes back three thousand years. The unique attraction for mathematics and the role it can play is best illustrated by the (truly) unexpurgated version of the Kama Sutra.

There are, unfortunately, no fully unexpurgated versions of the Kama Sutra in English. All translations have an important chapter omitted. Why? Too lascivious? Well you might think so if mathematics was your passion. These are hot mathematics problems. Mathematics problems? As the introduction to the Kama Sutra? Yes, indeed. There exist Sanscrit manuscripts which make reference to mathematics problems in the Kama Sutra, problems couched in the most delicate language and using sexual imagery. We have examples of similar problems from Aryabhata (c. 800AD), Mahavira (c. 850AD), and Bhaskara II (c. 1150AD).

One problem from Bhaskara II concerns a bee that falls into its lover's lotus flower, which closes upon him. Upon asking her to let him out, she responds that he must first solve the mathematics problem (the translation below is George Joseph's (1992) adaptation of Colebrook's original translation):

> From a swarm of bees, a number equalling the square root of half the total number of bees flew out to the lotus flowers. Soon after, 8/9 of the total swarm went to the same place. A male bee enticed by the fragrance of the lotus flew into it. But when it was inside the night fell, the lotus closed and the bee was caught inside. To its buzz, its consort responded anxiously from outside. Oh my beloved! How many bees are there in the swarm?

Here is a problem from Mahavira's *Ganitasarasamgraha* (again the translation is an adaptation by George Joseph (1992), this time from the original translation by Rangacharya):

One night in spring, a young lady was lovingly happy with her husband on the floor of a big mansion, white like the moon and situated in a pleasure garden with trees bent with flowers and fruits. The whole place was resonant with the sweet sounds of parrots, cuckoos and of bees which flew around intoxicated with the honey from the plentiful flowers. In the course of a "love quarrel" between the husband and wife, the lady's necklace came undone and the pearls scattered all around. One third of the pearls reached the maid-servant who was sitting nearby; one sixth fell on the bed; one half of what remained (and one half of what remained thereafter and again one half of what remained thereafter and so on, counting six times in all) were scattered everywhere. On the broken necklace it was found that there were 1161 pearls left. Oh my love, tell me the total number of pearls on the necklace.

Now what were these problems for? What part did problems like these have in a sex manual? The answer lies in the social context. At that time in India, the high society for whom the book was written was extremely well-educated in mathematics. Solving mathematical problems was a pleasure and delight that was part of the social scene. It could perhaps be compared with cryptic crosswords for some people nowadays.

So, what happens when a couple meet together after a long hard day at the office? Do they leap straight into bed? No, that would hardly be a romantic and sensitive way to behave. First it is necessary to reconnect as people, and what better way than to engage together in some gentle recreational activity, like, well, like solving a mathematics problem together. And if the mathematics problem is written in a suggestive way that might lead you on to more intimate things, so much the better.

We know these problems are not to be taken too seriously. The answers, for example, are not realistic. The answer to the Pearl Necklace problem is 148 608. That is a lot of pearls to count when there are better things to do. Joseph calls this a fantasy necklace and notes the fascination for very large numbers at that time—the content is more abstract than the erotic context suggests.

Mathematics and its role in society? There are clearly more possibilities than we ever dreamed about.

Chapter 7

WHAT IS MATHEMATICS? PHILOSOPHICAL COMMENTS

Abstract: This chapter addresses the issues that have been raised so far from a philosophical point of view. An extended metaphor of Middle Earth is used to describe a more relativistic view of mathematics.

Keywords: philosophy of mathematics, relativism, applications of mathematics

1.   MIDDLE EARTH

What about the Plato's ideal world inhabited by mathematical objects? Does it exist? Yes. Is a circle real? For sure. Is there such a thing as a prime number? Of course there is.

That world and the mathematical objects in it exist just like Tolkien's Middle Earth. Mathematics is a created world, a world of the human imagination, and, like Middle Earth, we can write about it, film it, become part of it in our minds and emotions. Also like Middle Earth mathematics has been expanded upon by others apart from Tolkien (despite his family's best attempts to preserve copyright), notably as Peter Jackson's film crew and actors gave more substance to the appearances and actions of the creatures and environment that make up that world. Mathematics has, it is true, a longer history, and many more screenwriters, but it can be thought of as an academic Middle Earth.

Can mathematics be compared to such a flight of imagination? Isn't there something much more contingent, much more true about the mathematical world than there is about Middle Earth? Once we have the number 1 and the number 2, then no mathematical Tolkien could have written anything other than $1 + 1 = 2$. Once we construct a circle and its diameter, and then draw a triangle on the diameter to a point on the circumference, it is not just geometric poetic licence that says that the angle at the circumference will be a right angle. And it is not just a muse's whisper that requires that right-angled triangle to have sides that obey the Pythagorean relationship. These things must be so.

The mistake is to think that this situation does not exist for Middle Earth. If you are a hobbit of Middle Earth, and you get yourself into deep trouble with the Forces of Evil, then, in your moment of dire need, lo, the Elves will come to your aid. It cannot be otherwise. For if it was otherwise it would not be Middle Earth!! It would be some other fantasy. The elements of Middle Earth were created in just such a relationship. Elves help humans: that characteristic is part of what Elves are. It was determined by their history (as written in the book) 2000 years before the time of Frodo and Sam and Bilbo Baggins. (Notice how we talk of these people as if they were real, with real histories, real names, real lives to be led—just as we talk of numbers and circles as if they were real objects that can be held, turned over, or combined with each other).

In the same way, if 1 + 1 does not equal 2, then we are not talking about the world of mathematics, we are in some other world. The number objects 1 and 2 were created into just the relationship embodied by 1 + 1 = 2. That is what mathematics is. Circles and triangles and angles were also created into their relationships.

But when Tolkien wrote *Lord of the Rings*, he had all the relationships and consequences worked out in advance. As the mathematicians write mathematics, the consequences of some of their supposed imaginative constructions are still being discovered, many are suspected but not yet proven, and still more are not yet known—or so the hundreds of budding mathematicians hope.

In order to properly understand the nature of mathematics, it is necessary to think of Lord of the Rings the computer game. Version 1 will closely resemble the book, and the relationships will be preserved intact, and the game will involve consequences of alliances, with some randomised luck thrown in: outcomes of individual battles; weather; perhaps the timing of the crumbling of the bridges in the Mines of Mordor. But then Version 2 will come out. A new, improved version. A few more subtleties. Perhaps some group of Elves will remember that they also had a 3000 year old pact with a group of Orcs who helped them in a time of need, and if, in the grand battle, this group of Elves come up against the Orcs then they might walk away. The writer of Version 2 will inject some of his or her own imagination, and may create some additional history for the characters. This will not be anything that contradicts Tolkien's original vision, but Tolkien did not have time nor space to write the complete history of Middle Earth, to describe each and every possible combination of relationship and circumstance. Plenty more can be written that is consistent with the copyright original.

The Version 2 Elves are not the same as Tolkien's Elves then? Yes and no. The computer game will be recognisable as Middle Earth, no contradictions will be involved, but the Elves will have evolved under new requirements. This has also happened in mathematics: Euclidean geometry with its circles and triangles and embedded relationships is now viewed as one of many possible geometries depending on the axioms. Non-Euclidean geometries, such as projective geometry, do not contradict Euclidean geometry, but evolved from it with new writers and new consequences as the literature of mathematics continued to be written.

Eventually, there will be Middle Earth Version 3. In this multi-dimensioned, multi-media extravaganza, Middle Earth is seen to be part of a greater world. Bilbo Baggins returns from his travels bringing new technologies and new perspectives. Middle Earth is a very special case of a universal fight between good and evil, tyranny and justice, truth and falsehood. The new technologies allow the Hobbits to understand more about what is right and to use this knowledge in their lives. The horizons for creating new beings and new relationships extends indefinitely, although Middle Earth remains intact as the literary historical origin of the edifice built upon it.

Now *that* is like mathematics. The words 'dimension', 'technology', 'special case' and 'new relationships' were used in the previous paragraph with intent. The parallels I leave for the reader.

The idea embodied in calling mathematics Middle Earth is not original. Wittgenstein seems to be saying the same thing when he says that a mathematical statement is a prescription or a rule (1956, I–30, 33). That is, every mathematical statement is saying "This is how it should be if you want to be in a mathematical world"—just as Tolkein's descriptions of Orcs can be seen as statements of what certain things are like in the Middle Earth.

Middle Earth is also a braid with many origins. If we regard Tolkein's novel as an allegory on good and evil, then it is one of many such allegories arising in many different cultures. They exist alongside each other, borrow from each other, can be discussed in relation to each other. This is parallel to mathematics being seen as a QRS-system alongside other QRS-systems.

Even within Tolkein's creation there could be many fibres, as copycat writers pick up his themes, or abridged versions for young children or radio plays emerge, or a modern writer picks up an incident in the story and creates a new work.

Notice also that Middle Earth bears more than a passing resemblance to our experiential reality. We recognise the practical level (the characters ride horses, live in houses, and suffer the weather), the contextual level (things fall under gravity, landscapes are earth-like), and the human level (the morals, emotions, and physical constraints like wounds and illness are all familiar). Tolkein's world is consistent and speaks to us about our experience. Just like mathematics.

2.   MATHEMATICAL WORLDS

The evidence from language, and other reflections, have led us to the idea of a braid of many strands. The strand that is NUC-mathematics has been discussed above. What about the others? These different strands have sometimes been referred to as different mathematical worlds.

The idea that there can be several mathematical worlds is far from new. In Western literature, it was described by Oswald Spengler (1926, 1956). His grand conception was that a mathematic (singular) was a feature of each cultural era (like art or architecture), and that all such features grow, flourish and decline contemporaneously in every culture. Spengler focussed on the conception of number. Number, he claimed, is a representation of thought, of a conception of the world. The difference between the Classical idea and the modern Western idea of number, for example, is that number is regarded as measure-ment in the former, and as a relation in the latter. The important point made by Spengler is that this is not a development, but in each era there is a destruction of the concept of number of the previous era, and the generation of a new one. Eighty years after Spengler, the question of whether mathematics develops gradually, or whether old concepts die and are replaced by new concepts, is still being debated (Gillies, 1992).

Mathematical worlds are also discussed by Sal Restivo (Restivo, 1983, 1992; Restivo, Van Bendegem, & Fischer, 1993). He believes that "all talk about mathematics is social talk" based on the Marxist view that all human activities are social activities and social products. Restivo notes two interpretations of the relationship between mathematics and culture. The weak view is that mathematics is a social and cultural phenomenon, so that mathematical ideas and activities vary from culture to culture, and that the results of the various cultural mathematics together make up world mathematics. The weak view is adequately demonstrated by examining mathematics from different historical periods and cultures. The strong view challenges the idea that all cultural traditions in mathematics contribute to the same mathematics. Rather it assumes different mathematics' and incommensurability between them.

This leads Restivo to describe 'math worlds' (Restivo, Van Bendegem, & Fischer, 1993, p. 249–50). He notes that pure mathematical concepts appear objective when they are communicated, hence mathematics is a social world of people communicating about their ideas—agreeing, disagreeing, arguing. Mathematics is not a world of triangles, symbols, rules of argument; it is a world of networks of people talking about ideas. The social practice generates the objects and the results of mathematics through naming and arguing.

Both Spengler's and Restivo's views are culturally based and refer as much to the nature of the surrounding culture as they do to the nature of the mathematics in the worlds being described. Can we get closer in to the mathematics?

Do different mathematical worlds mean, as asked in the Introduction, that mathematics as an academic discipline is somehow different in different parts of the world? A bridge designed using mathematical theory surely stands (or falls) in the same way independently of the country it is built in, or of the language of the person who solved the equations of its design? Surely $1 + 1 = 2$ in Alaska, Nigeria, Tahiti and Singapore?

Think about the bridge for a moment. The technical part of building a bridge involves resolving the forces that might make it fall down. This is largely an empirical matter—does it fall down or not? In 2003 the remains of a Bronze Age bridge was found in Wessex, England. There were no mathematicians around in England during the Bronze Age, according to histories of the subject, but clearly there were effective bridgebuilders. There were mathematicians around in 25BC to help build the Pont Saint-Martin, one of the oldest surviving bridges, but their mathematics would not have included the techniques that would be used today in the same circumstances. One wonders what mathematics was being used in 1756 by William Edwards, the builder of the Pontypridd Bridge. He had to reconstruct the bridge several times before he got the rise-to-span ratio correct: an expensive trial and error procedure.

The point here is that the mathematics is how we make sense of the technology we need. The experiences of bridge-building, the talking about these experiences and what ideas explain them, the use of mathematical techniques that have been developed in other situations, lead mathematicians to develop effective ways of describing bridges before they are built and communicating about whether they are likely to stay built (that is, effective ways of designing them). A bridge does not stay up because of the mathematics. It stays up because it is built effectively. Mathematics is one way of discussing what "built effectively" means.

So, yes, a bridge designed using a mathematical theory stands (or falls) in the same way independently of the country it is built in, or of the language of the person who solved the equations of its design. But many mathematical theories may adequately describe why the bridge stands or falls. The techniques of engineering mathematics are wonderfully detailed and can cope with a vast range of potential bridges—bigger and bigger as the mathematics and the materials develop. The mathematical theory used to design the bridge stands (or falls) on the success of the bridge—this statement is not the same as saying there is only one possible mathematical theory.

Notice that the "correctness" of the mathematical theory is something of an empirical matter. If the bridge falls down then the builder needs to think again (like William Edwards). More accurately, the correctness or appropriateness of the application of the theory is an empirical matter. What about the pure mathematical theory itself? Surely it is right or wrong.

Hence we come to $1 + 1 = 2$. Surely the equation is correct in Alaska, Nigeria, Tahiti and Singapore? I need some help here, and I am calling on Wittgenstein.

3.   WITTGENSTEINIAN MATHEMATICAL WORLDS

Many different writers have made commentaries on Wittgenstein's writing. I prefer Shanker's (1987) interpretation. He notes that Wittgenstein was concerned that mathematical philosophy should look at how mathematical expressions are used, and at the logic of such expressions, not at whether mathematical expressions refer to anything "real" or not. When this is done, it becomes clear that mathematical expressions are rules, not descriptions. Mathematics is neither a description of the world nor a useful science-like theory: it is a system, the statements of which are the rules which must be used to make meaning within that system.

Grammatical analysis reveals that sometimes we use mathematical expressions as if they were part of familiar syntactical domains, and Wittgenstein believes that this is the source of traditional philosophical argument. For example, treating '15' as a thing, and its divisors as discoveries to be made is a Platonist/realist domain; or treating a mathematical 'group' as an arbitrary construction which could have been otherwise is a constructivist domain. At different times either of these grammatical similarities seem more appropriate. However, we cannot thereby argue that one or the other is correct. Mathematical syntax has is its own domain to be analysed for its logical grammar irrespective of how, or when, it is similar to a Platonist or to a constructivist domain.

Let me note again that English, the language we have come to use for mathematics, tends to make mathematical ideas into objects. We talk of mathematical objects because that is what the English language makes available for talking, but it is just a way of talking. Bishop (1988, 1990) identifies the objectifying tendency of mathematics to be one of the values inherent in the subject. For NUC-mathematics, this is because of its Indo-European linguistic roots. A non-objectifying mathematics is possible.

Wittgenstein claims that mathematical statements are normative descriptions of how the world is seen, of what is meant by being intelligible. We cannot have 'intelligible' communities who divide by zero, or who calculate 24 × 30 as 712, or who measure differently, because such communities would not see numbers and counting as the same sort of thing or activity as we do, thus they would not be intelligible. $1 + 1 = 2$ is always the case because this is the standard of the correct use of numbers in the discourse of the mathematical world we inhabit. That is how we agree to count. It does not make sense to say that $1 + 1 \neq 2$ (Shanker, 1987, p. 303).

People in a different mathematical world will not be talking about the same idea if they use the symbols '1', '+', '=', '2' and do not accept that $1 + 1 = 2$. The clash of different mathematical worlds is obvious when the same word is used to describe different ideas. We have discussed what happens when mathematicians have different views on continuity or probability, or different cultures have different views on navigation or shape. Any community or culture is free to make its own sense of the world. Mathematics is the name we give to how it chooses to express the sense of quantity, relationships, or space.

Rotman (1987, p. 2) makes the same point with respect to symbols, and similarly rejects the idea of mathematical things being prior to mathematical signs. It is not the case that mathematics was "there", was then "discovered and named", and then remained unchanged.

He compares mathematics with art and finance. We have "the natural but mistaken notion that a painting is simply a depiction and money a representation of some economic reality". That is to say, we often treat pictures as if they showed us reality: "That picture captures the colour of the ocean on a stormy day", we might say, but actually it just invokes in us the sense we have when viewing a stormy ocean, and would not do that if we had never seen a stormy ocean. The lie to pictures representing reality is most clearly found in those pictures of impossible images, Escher's etching of the never-ending steps being a good example.

Similarly, we treat money as if it represented some actual commodity, when what it actually represents is "value", and what that means changes with our actions. This is clear when we say things like: "Bill Gates lost half a billion dollars on the stock market this week". This does not represent any actual change in things that he owns.

It is the same with mathematical signs. Rotman focuses on the role of zero, because it demonstrates that numbers do not represent any thing. If we regarded numbers as representing a reality, even the reality of our action of counting, then zero is a problem, since it represents the absence of that reality. As soon as we allow zero to be a number, then we must give up the idea that some thing is being represented—by zero, or by any other number. Numbers are seen to be signs that we use. They are not things, nor do they represent any thing. "Numbers signify the activity of one who counts" (Rotman, 1987, pp. 8–9).

Both Rotman and Wittgenstein make the point that mathematical symbols and expressions are made and remade repeatedly. These are not individually created, but are public, culturally dependent forms of communication.

If mathematics is the way mathematicians talk, then the cultural influences on that talk (the language of discourse, the meanings of words and symbols at the time of the talk) create different mathematics. If mathematics is a set of normative rules, then they could have been different. We accept different rules of grammar in different languages, and the other ways of talking about the world that those languages generate.

Another mind-game. I once spent some time in Guiyang in Guizhou province in southern China where my wife was teaching English. There I met an American linguist who was studying the indigenous Miao language, a member of the Hmong-Mien family of languages. I asked him whether his American-learned linguistic theory was adequate to describe everything he found in the Miao language. He replied that yes it was, although he sometimes had to bend it a bit, or create new categories within that theory.

Now the mind-game. I then asked whether he thought that a hypothetical Miao linguist, who had studied linguistics built up around Hmong-Mien languages, or Sino-Tibetan languages in general, would be able to use his linguistics to describe American English. The reply was predictable: yes, but probably that linguistics would have to be bent a little. What I now asked was this: after the American had twisted his linguistics to fit Miao, and the Miao had twisted his linguistics to fit American English, would the resulting two linguistic systems be the same? My intuition (and my friend agreed) is that the answer is no. Linguistics can be different. Mathematical worlds can similarly be different.

As Shanker points out (1987, p. 319), the possibility of different mathematical worlds does not mean that mathematics is arbitrary, and thereby opens the way for mathematical anarchy. We are free to construct the grammatical rules of mathematics, but the grammar comes before truth, it determines what makes sense. The rules therefore cannot be true or false. Neither predetermined meaning, nor reality, can be used to justify such rules.

An example that shows that predetermined meaning does not justify the rules of mathematical discourse is when anomalies or contradictions emerge in mathematical investigations. The most famous of these are the paradoxes of self-reference that Bertrand Russell attempted to resolve, but more commonly known as the barber paradox: if a barber shaves all those who do not shave themselves, then who shaves the barber himself? Mathematicians' attempts to satisfactorily define concepts such as sets to resolve the difficulty get tangled up in contradictions and impossibilities within their own frame of reference. Meanings of mathematical ideas evolve. That is to say, the grammar of mathematics, what is accepted as making sense, evolves, as we communicate more and more about mathematical ideas.

A final point about Wittgenstein's mathematical worlds. What happens when different mathematical systems meet? Wittgenstein's answer is that there are no 'gaps' in mathematics. Each system is complete at any moment. It is not waiting to be added to with new mathematics. Thus (Shanker, 1987, p. 329), any connection between two worlds is not in the same space as either of the worlds. The interconnections are not waiting to be discovered. We choose whether or not to make connections between systems, and if we do then the connections create a new system.

4.   MATHEMATICS AND EXPERIENCE

We have looked at bridges (applied mathematics) and $1 + 1 = 2$ (pure mathematics). Let us say a little more about the relationship between the two. When do numbers apply to the real world?

What we forget most of the time is that numbers are mathematical ways of talking, they are not aspects of the world. In some situations numbers (as they have been constructed in mathematical talk) are useful models of the real world, and sometimes the ways we use numbers mathematically do not fit at all to the quantitative aspects of the world we wish to talk about.

We saw this happening in the story about fractions. The "rules" for being sensible with numbers, including fractions, do not apply in every situation in which we wish to represent quantity by one number divided by another. It is possible to make the rules apply by putting alternative interpretations on the word "add" and then using the rules as normal. This example highlights the relationship between the mathematical world and reality. I can make the mathematical world apply by interpreting the situation—mathematics does not just apply automatically. It is not real. Nor is the situation that fits the rules (in the fractions case adding pieces of pies) more mathematically correct or privileged than the other situations.

The next example shows how we move between contexts within mathematics without acknowledging their differences. First, consider counting a large stock of books. Let us say that there are 25 cartons of 50 books. How many books altogether? We know that the mathematical way of talking called multiplication can apply to this situation: multiply the two numbers together: $25 \times 50 = 1250$ books.

Now consider the measurement of rectangular areas. We also regard this as a matter of multiplying two numbers representing the length and breadth of the rectangle. Thus an area 25 metres by 50 metres is calculated : $25 \times 50 = 1250$ square metres. But these are not numbers in the same way that 25 is the number of cartons of books. For area, the 25 and 50 represent measurements which have errors. (Mathematically we take account of this by modelling them as Real numbers. The number of books and cartons are Whole numbers, or possibly fractions in the case of the cartons).

We only know measurements within a certain accuracy. It is extremely difficult to measure anything to four significant digits, let alone five or six. In this example, giving normal rounding off, 25 and 50 could represent values as high as 25.4 and 54 or as low as 24.5 and 45, respectively. Multiplying these maximum or minimum values gives areas of 1371.6 sq. metres and 1102.5 sq. metres, so the range of possible actual areas varies by over 260 sq. metres, about 20%.

We explain away the discrepancy by a theory of errors—or in a mathematics textbook we just say "an area of exactly 25 metres by 50 metres" which is nonsense. We act as if we can interpret both situations by the same meaning of number, and disguise the fact that they are fundamentally different conceptions.

Their similarity is sufficient for a large range of practical situations, of course, but it can lead us into trouble. If we come to think of multiplication as the same as these applications, then we will have problems when we multiply negative numbers.

5.   RECURRENT HISTORY: BACHELARD

We have examined mathematical objects, and seen that they are possible creations within a mathematical world generated by a social community. But what about objectivity? Is there no way of judging between different mathematical worlds on some objective basis? Is there no way to dismiss as nonsense some mathematical worlds that purport to make sense of our experience of quantity, relationships and space?

First, how do we explain that, historically, our idea of what constitutes rationality has changed? The French philosopher Gaston Bachelard, writing in the 1930s, makes an attempt. He describes a historically relative notion of objectivity which allows for changing conceptions of mathematical objects and of rationality, (see Smith, 1982; Tiles, 1984).

For Bachelard, mathematics allows us to create new realities using new structures of knowledge. Bachelard's key idea is that objectivity is an ideal rather than a reality. At any one time we may think that we see clearly how things are, or that we know how to discover the truth, or that we understand what makes a proof. However these ideas change over time, that is, the sense of objectivity is illusory. Objectivity is not, however, nothing. Conceptions of mathematics at different times depend on changing notions of rationality, each successive change being regarded as being more objective than the last. There is a progression towards a better, and then a still better, understanding of the things that must be taken into account to get an objective view.

A consequence of this analysis is that there are many different historical standpoints from which to view mathematics, each of which is correct *at that time* and each of which explains previous views. Each such view gains its apparent objectivity because of the wide agreement amongst mathematicians about the view, and because it is seen to arise from previous views and encompass them. This historical explanation allows for the development of mathematics over time, and for the changing, creative nature of mathematical ideas, while retaining the objectivity required of the discipline.

Bachelard's idea is called recurrent history because history keeps being re-evaluated in the light of present knowledge: mathematicians look at their own practices and conceptions in the light of other practices and conceptions; modify, reinterpret, discard, or adopt particular practices; and retain the knowledge of how and why this was done as part of their mathematical understanding. These changes are themselves the subject of critical reflection when further advances are made.

I suggest that a similar situation can exist between contemporaneous mathematical worlds. Mathematicians from different worlds can look at their own practices and conceptions in the light of the practices and conceptions of other worlds; modify, reinterpret, discard, or adopt particular practices; and retain the knowledge of how and why this was done as part of their mathematical understanding. In the same way that we do not reject as wrong historical practices and conceptions (only see them as consistent within their historical context and use that knowledge to inform the present), so too could mathematicians from each world acknowledge the other mathematics within their context and use the knowledge to reflect on their own.

If this is true, how is it that not all mathematicians acknowledge that this process has gone on? Mathematicians have a consciousness of change, of what motivated particular thoughts, new ideas and so on, but they are not necessarily conscious that this is a culturally relative process. Most mathematicians regard their subject as universal and from their point of view it is. If opposing ideas arise, whether internally or from a different mathematical world, then there is eventually a cognitive shift to accommodate the clash of domains. When this is achieved the sense of universality returns. It is only when this process is reflected upon that we see the relativity of the past situation. Universality, like Bachelard's concept of objectivity, is an (unattainable) ideal that guides mathematical development. It is illusory in that any claim to universality may be challenged by an awareness of a different culturally-based view; but it is real because, at any given time for any particular person, there is a complete explanation for the domain of mathematical concepts.

Bachelard's description of recurrent history is helpful when we want to describe different mathematical worlds. Particular conceptions of mathematics begin and end, but also live on, in the critical role played by the historical definition of present conceptions. The end occurs when a new conception encompasses the past ones and resolves any conflict that has arisen. Culturo-mathematical worlds are also temporary in the sense that they end when a new world arises out of two meeting ones. However each world lives on in the critical role played by the conflicts of the meeting.

Mathematical practices are quickly accommodated, and can usually be transported across cultural boundaries without much difficulty because they are very generalised, have broad areas of applicability, and can therefore adapt to a wide range of activities. However the interplay between mathematical worlds is not so visible because the resolution of conflicting conceptions gets played out through many practices. This explains why mathematical conceptions of minor cultures become colonised: the mathematical conception with the wider range of applicability will accommodate different practices more readily.

6.   UNIVERSAL OR RELATIVE

I will try to sum up where we have got to philosophically by dealing directly with the question about universality and relativity. Where does the evidence from language lead me? Is mathematics universal, or is it relative? My answer, predictably, is both. It depends what you mean. I can see two senses in which mathematics is universal, and two senses in which it is relative.

The first universal sense arises from the fact that, if you are in a particular mathematical world, then it is possible to look at another mathematical world and see it in your terms. For example, Bishop (1988) identifies six pre-mathematical practices which are present in every culture: counting, measuring, locating, designing, playing, and explaining. Bishop is not saying that these activities are equivalently defined in every culture; he is saying that he can identify in any culture activities which come under each of these headings as far as he is concerned. This leaves open the question as to whether numbers exist in some real sense because everyone counts, or triangles exist because everyone designs; or the continuum exists because everyone measures. These 'objects' could be conceptual tools with no existence beyond the conceiver. This sense of universality does not imply a Platonist reality.

The second sense in which mathematics is universal results from the fact that, if you acknowledge mathematics at all, then you must acknowledge conventional NUC-mathematics. For, if you don't, then it is difficult to justify your use of the label 'mathematics'. Mathematics exists as a knowledge category, recognised by a very large proportion of humans in every culture. To call something else mathematics, is not making sense of the use of that word. NUC-mathematics is universal because it is part of the meaning of 'mathematics'.

These senses of universal mathematics do not mean that the subject is static. A person may hold a differing view of mathematics from the conventional one to the extent that a debate may take place through which mathematics may change its conventional meaning. Development is possible. For this to occur, however, there must be one of two situations. Either the unconventional viewer acknowledges that the conventional view has legitimacy and the onus is on them to convince others that a change is justified (for example, Joseph's writings on non-European aspects of mathematics (1991)); or there may be more than one community of convention, mutually acknowledged by the other as having a right to the debate (such as the communities of standard and non-standard analysis, or Bayesian and Frequentist statisticians).

Now relativity. The first sense in which mathematics is relative is that it can change. This change is more than just an evolutionary building on what has gone before, it involves revolutionary change in the sense that fundamental ways of thinking can change (see Gillies, 1992, Section 2.3). Completely different mathematical concepts, which are subsumable neither by existing ones, nor by some new, overarching generalisation, are possible. In other words, a new mathematical concept may arise which radically changes existing mathematics because it cannot be integrated into mathematics as presently understood in any other way.

The second sense in which mathematics is relative is that mathematics is not the only way to see the world, nor is it the only way to see those aspects of the world having to do with number, relationships, or space. Other people may see things that I might call mathematical in entirely different terms.

To summarise: if we are to ask whether there is, in fact, another mathematics equal in power to NUC-mathematics, then the answer is no. On the other hand, if we are to ask whether mathematics could have been different, then the answer is yes.

Historically, the line of progress of mathematics could have been otherwise. We cannot know what theory of mathematics we might now have, nor whether this hypothetical theory would be more comprehensive, more sophisticated, more applicable, or 'better' by any other criterion. It is not possible to completely rewrite history (Lakatos, 1978).

The sociology of mathematics will help us identify how divergent ideas may have changed the path of mathematical development: to identify the turning points and decision points; to specify the socio-cultural conditions which determined particular paths; and to trace paths as far as possible. The anthropology of mathematics will help us explore the existence of other paths and other mathematical worlds (even in embryonic form). Both of those have a historical orientation. An ethnomathematician's task is to explore—in the present—the consequences of different worlds for mathematics: first to understand where they were/are leading, and then to reflect on them mathematically.

The lack of more than one contemporary, sophisticated mathematics does not imply the universality of the one we know—it only contributes to our feeling of its truth. There is potential for divergent mathematical development, which I call contemporary relativity.

7.   EVIDENCE, REFLECTIONS, & CONSEQUENCES

We have used the evidence from the language of everyday mathematical talk to reflect upon mathematics, and have come to some far-reaching suggestions about the nature of mathematics. One of these conclusions is that mathematics and language evolved together. Does this mean that we can suggest things about language and linguistics from this evidence?

Questions of whether languages evolved from a common proto-language, and whether there are linguistically universal concepts, are intricately tied up with the arguments of this book. For example, if it is argued that mathematics develops differently in different languages, then it might still be possible to have a single, universal mathematics if there are some things that are linguistically the same, no matter what language you speak. Mathematics could be exactly those things that are universal.

I believe that the weight of evidence presented in this book opposes such an idea. To the extent that we regard language as the cultural expression of a world view, there appear to be quantitative, spatial, and relational aspects of some world views that are not essentially the same. We do, indeed, still talk of 'quantitative' aspects of each world view—but this is just our way of talking and making sense of the differences we see.

What about whether different languages evolved from a single common language? If there are such different conceptions of mathematics embedded in languages, then this is evidence that all languages did not evolve from one language—or if they did then it was before some elementary quantitative, spatial, and relationship conceptions were formed. The latter possibility seems unlikely, therefore the mathematical evidence suggests that some languages must have evolved independently.

However, I am not a linguist, and the debate about such things contains much more evidence than that from mathematics (Chomsky, 1998; Pinker, 1994).

Part I of this book presents some evidence to illustrate that mathematical ideas are represented in fundamentally different ways in the everyday talk of different languages. It also explored how some of these could evolve in different directions or into different structures in mathematics. The idea being put forward is that there could be different mathematical worlds, or that mathematics could have evolved in another way from the one that we know.

Part II examines the consequences for mathematics. It describes the origins and evolution of mathematics from a stance which accepts the possibility of other mathematical worlds. Further illustrations are given, and evidence and supporting views of others from both the history, anthropology, and sociology of mathematics is presented. What emerges is a picture of mathematics as a plaited braid of many strands, that merge and split, fold back and tangle—but a braid in which there is no 'one way' unless you are looking from inside one of the strands.

This picture leads to some philosophical reflections about mathematics, particularly to the writings of Wittgenstein as interpreted by Shanker, and to a way of conceiving both the universality and the relativity of mathematics as meaningful.

The final section of the book looks at the consequences of this point of view for mathematics education. The evidence from different languages makes us think again about how we might approach teaching, particularly to students whose language is not Indo-European, or not the same as our own. We must also think about what it is that we are teaching, and the underlying experiences and dispositions that will lead to high levels of creativity and application in the mathematical and information sciences and their applications.

To finish this section, let us remind ourselves that what has been said has been said before. The idea that language and mathematical thought are inextricably linked is not new, nor is the recognition of the potential for new mathematics embedded in other languages. Benjamin Whorf has already been quoted. He also said (1956, p. 245):

> …an important field for working out new order systems, akin to, yet not identical with, present mathematics, lies in more penetrating investigation than has yet been made of languages remote in type from our own.

PART III

IMPLICATIONS FOR MATHEMATICS EDUCATION

Chapter 8

LEARNING MATHEMATICS

Abstract: The conclusions of the book are examined for their implications for mathematics education, and an argument is made for attention to be paid to the communicative aspects of mathematics during its development in schools. This includes more exploration at all levels of education, and the importance of informing students of the nature of mathematics. Some notes on assessment are made.

Keywords: communication mathematics teaching, meta-mathematics, explorations in mathematics

1. CONCLUSIONS THROUGH EDUCATIONAL EYES

Learning mathematics has been an enigma for many thousands of years. On the one hand it seems so straight forward. Counting things feels natural, and young children often find numbers playful, reciting them as songs, for example. We all have adequate spatial intuitions. We find our way around our familiar environment without apparent effort. Those living in a city easily make complex routing decisions, and those living in the country develop a directional sense that is reliable and automatic. In many activities we perform mathematical tasks with ease: we intuitively estimate the trajectory of balls in many sports; weavers and sewers and designers manipulate patterns and shapes in sophisticated ways; people build model or real houses and boats that are robust and balanced; and the ever present money transactions in modern life are routinely handled with efficiency.

On the other hand, mathematics classrooms have been places of fear and puzzlement for many, probably since they first appeared in China around 1000BC (Swetz, 1974). They have received bad press throughout literature, and Math Phobia has now become a buzz-word

(Burns, 1998; Clawson, 1991; Tobias, 1995). Many people experience the mathematics classroom as a place of pleasure and wonder, but even this positive aspect is often turned by society into a negative one. Those for whom formal mathematics education is easy and a pleasure are routinely transformed into oddities or nerds.

The enigma of learning mathematics, and the best teaching methods for it, have been discussed explicitly since at least Greek times when Socrates put forward his method. What light can we shed on this enigma by reflecting on language and mathematics? What are the implications for education of the conclusions of Parts I and II? After looking through educational eyes at the conclusions already reached about mathematics, this chapter discusses what our reflections tell us about the nature of mathematics learning in general. I suggest a conclusion about the role of abstraction that is at odds with general thinking, and make some comments about the role of mathematical play and creativity. We finish by examining implications that can be drawn for formal classroom teaching.

The second chapter in this section discusses two particular language contexts. I argue that multilingual environments are a rich source of learning rather than ones filled with problems, and then I discuss the particular situation of indigenous education. Indigenous groups are faced with an interesting dilemma. They learn mathematics in a distinct cultural-linguistic context—how can they study an international subject while retaining the integrity of a minority world view?

In order to keep focussed on the conclusions that have been generated from the evidence from language, I summarise the five main conclusions.

The most important conclusion is that mathematics and language develop together. Historically this has been so, with each of these two areas of human activity affecting the other. It continues to be so, as new language and mathematics is generated in new areas of human interest: computer environments; space exploration; biological modelling; the mathematics of finance. The co-development of mathematics and language happens at both a macro- and a micro-level. At a macrolevel they both respond to social and political demands. At the microlevel, the vocabulary and syntax of mathematical discourse responds to that of the language being spoken (and the world view represented therein), as well as to the mathematical needs. The discourse may then affect the direction of mathematical development.

The educational perspective on this conclusion concerns the development of mathematical ideas in an individual. To what extent is the historical link with language also present in personal mathematical development? At first there does not seem to be a necessary connection between the two, but two threads of argument suggest otherwise. The evidence strongly suggests that mathematics as it has evolved does have strong ties with particular language characteristics, and that these need to be established for an individual in some way or other if this mathematics is to be easily understood. Also, the evidence about the difference between mathematical discourse and everyday language means that, even if your language is consonant with NUC-mathematics, there are still changes in your language that need to be made to correctly understand, communicate, and use mathematical ideas.

A second conclusion, related to the first, is the idea that mathematics arises after, not before, human activity, in response to human thinking and communicating about quantity, relationships, and space within particular socio-cultural environments. An educational perspective asks whether (or in what way) socio-cultural context (including language) might be important for understanding a mathematical concept. For example, does the gambling origins of probability theory mean that an understanding of gambling is necessary (or helpful) for statistical education? Will a child who has only experienced probability in the more Bayesian environment of predicting the outcome of a sporting event, have difficulty conceptualising long-run Frequentist ideas? My view is that these are likely to be important considerations in mathematical learning.

A third conclusion of Parts I and II is that mathematics could be different. A corollary of this is that there are still many undeveloped mathematical ideas. This statement does not only refer to advanced level research mathematics. There are still undeveloped ideas in pre-formalised mathematics, elementary mathematics, and at every subsequent level.

The educational perspective on this conclusion is that mathematics is far from a complete and established set of concepts and relationships that can be presented to anyone learning the subject. Nor is mathematics a body of ideas that all children will come to discover in a natural way, even if they are given appropriate activities. At every level there are alternatives to be acknowledged and the possibility of exploring them. The depth of this conclusion cannot be over-emphasised. It is not just a question of different techniques of multiplication—it is a question of what operations are possible and sensible at all, or, at an even more basic level, the possible different conceptions of quantity that can exist in a formal way. The conclusion means not only that a mathematics classroom should be open to unconventional mathematics, but also that it must exhibit unconventional ideas, particularly if we wish students to understand what the human activity we call mathematics is all about. A further impli cation is that conventional mathematics must be explained as just that—conventional.

A fourth conclusion is that mathematics is created by communicating, that is, mathematics arises within the communication. I am not just saying that mathematics arises because of the need to communicate, nor just that mathematics is recorded by communication (writing it down as a journal article, for example). Mathematics is created in the act of communication—even the mathematics that is reportedly created in intuitive flashes of an individual when they are alone. The ideas of such flashes do not become mathematics until they are formalised and related to other ideas—until they become part of a system.

An educational perspective asks whether this implies that mathematics is learned through communication. This perspective also focuses on the nature of the communication, and the role played by different people in it. More critical, however, is the idea that mathematical knowledge is therefore never finished, never completed. Whatever understanding a learner reaches is always an understanding of the communication that has just happened—further communication will generate further mathematical understanding.

The most fundamental conclusion of this book is that each language contains its own mathematical world. The worlds may be implicit, of small scope, and/or undeveloped, but these worlds exist—they are not just rudimentary versions of conventional mathematics, nor are they simple, unformalised mathematics. These worlds represent systems of meaning concerned with quantity, relationships, or space, and are, in some sense, incommensurable with NUC-mathematics.

An educational theorist, faced with this conclusion, is likely to ask for justification that one world is the subject of curricular attention while another is not. They are unlikely to accept as a sole answer that one world is more extensive, or more developed. Rather they will want to know about the relationship between this world and the particular learners for whom the curriculum applies. They will evaluate the justification on educational criteria (for example the overall aims of education) as much as on mathematical grounds. And they will ask whether one world needs to be exclusive of others. This issue is especially important for indigenous mathematics education.

A more direct educational issue relating to mathematical worlds is the psychological question of the extent to which an individual is wedded to one world view, and whether (or how) this will affect their understanding of another world view. This question has long been asked by mathematics educators as they search for answers to the differential performance of particular groups in various educational environments. It will be obvious to the reader that my view is that learners are more affected by their world view than is commonly acknowledged.

There are three further issues related to mathematical language that can be viewed from an educational perspective. Mathematical language change is in the direction of more similarity. In other words, different languages are evolving to express QRS ideas in ways that are more and more the same. Is this good for education because it means that there is more uniformity and less need to accommodate differences, or is it detrimental for education because it means that variety and versatility are being lost?

Mathematical language (not just mathematics) evolves from the physical and social environment. To what extent does the everyday meaning and environmental origin of mathematical vocabulary and discourse interfere with or enhance mathematical meaning? Teachers need to take into account the conditions under which the everyday meaning of a mathematical word can contribute to the development of mathematical understanding.

Finally, mathematical language is more consonant with some languages, and less consonant with others. In what ways is this a problem (for example, speakers of less consonant languages might find mathematical constructions difficult), and in what ways is this an advantage (for example, a wide difference between natural language and mathematical discourse may emphasise the particular nature of mathematical discourse and reduce the interferences mentioned in the previous paragraph).

This summary of the main conclusions and what they mean from an educational point of view sets the scene for a look at mathematical learning, mathematical teaching, and mathematics education in the particular contexts of multilingual and indigenous peoples' education.

2.   BECOMING A BETTER GOSSIP

I take the hand of my three-year-old granddaughter as we jump down the cobbled steps in the narrow street of the old town. Jump-"one". Jump-"two". She knows this game, and we count for a while. Then I start again: jump-"two". Silence. Jump-"four". "You missed three, Pa-Bill." "I don't like three," I say. The inevitable "why" and I make it clear that it is part of the game: "let's pretend", I say, and that is enough, she knows how to pretend. Soon we have a rhythm: jump-"two", "you missed one"; jump-"four", "you missed three"; jump-"six", "you missed five"; and so on. She did not, as it happened, demand to take the lead with her own sequence, but I would not have been surprised. Young children can play games better than most, and can generate complex games at the drop of a hat, remembering and changing rules as they go along.

For the two of us, what had been the counting numbers became just a sequence of words that were part of a game. We were not counting any more, since 2, 4, 6, ... is not how we record single jumps, we were game-playing. We were at the very beginnings of talking about relations between numbers as abstract objects, as opposed to their practical application as recording the act of counting.

Young children also understand relationships between people, and can articulate them, often embarrassingly. It is said that a two-year-old is the best guru you can have. Watch one go around a room full of adults and systematically elicit reactions from every one. Sibling rivalries and playground positioning are more evidence. This is not to say that their awareness is conscious or their actions deliberate—but at some level young children understand complex human relation-ships. Why not mathematical ones?

It is noted in Part II that Keith Devlin describes mathematics as the same sort of activity as gossip. That is, mathematics is talk about relationships, but at a higher level of abstraction: it is about relationships between mathematical ideas, not between people. The important thing he notes is that it is the same kind of talk (Devlin, 2001, p. 244):

> ... [A] mathematician is someone for whom mathematics is a soap opera. ... I am not referring to the mathematical community but to mathematics itself. The 'characters' in the mathematical soap opera are not people but mathematical objects ... . The facts and relationships .. are not births and deaths, marriages and love affairs, but mathematical facts and relationships. ... The secret of all those people who seem to be "good at maths" [is] not that they have different brains. It's just that they have found a way to use a standard issue brain in a slightly different way.

Given that mathematics is created in communication, that mathematics happens in the act of gossiping, then the trick to doing mathematics is to do what everyone has no difficulty doing, but do it with abstract ideas. There is good evidence that young children do know about relationships and act on that knowledge. There is also good evidence that they can play with relationships in an abstract way: they play games with rules all the time, and they both articulate and manipulate rules explicitly. Furthermore they can play games with rules about mathematical ideas also. Children do not need to have 3 follow 2, they do not need to have the 'correct' number of objects to refer to. They can suspend their dependence on reality if that is part of the game. All young children can do mathematics in this very real sense. All older people can too.

A relevant question to be asked is how this ability can be nurtured. How can I go about increasing my ability to think and act mathematically? A likely answer is to practice 'gossiping' with abstractions as often as possible, or, if I am responsible for young children, to play such abstract games whenever the opportunity arises. We need to establish a wide base of real experiences from which to abstract, and we should develop a large background of gossiping about abstractions. Advanced mathematical development is unlikely to happen until there have been a lot of abstraction experiences.

In the light of this conclusion it is interesting to note that a common educational response for children who are having difficulty with school mathematics is to give them more concrete problems, to reduce the abstraction by giving problems for which they can refer to real world situations. This strategy does increase the base of real experience, but it does nothing about increasing the base of abstract activity that is also needed to appreciate formal mathematics. In many cases sufficient real experience is already present, and so a better strategy would be to undertake abstract activity in an appropriate way—that is, at a level of game-playing rather than within formal mathematics.

A reflection on young children's development of the ability to gossip about abstract things is suggested by Oliver Sacks' (1991) book about sign language. Sacks presents the evidence that the groundwork for the ability to understand language as a concept is laid down before age eight. In other words, if a child has not experienced language by this age, if, say, they have been isolated from speaking human contact, then they will never really 'get it'. Even if they subsequently join a language community, they may learn to communicate, but will never properly develop linguistic skills. To the extent that mathematics is like language as a cognitive function, we can infer that the same is true: if there is no experiential base of abstract gossip before some early age, perhaps it will never fully develop. Could this be the key to Math Phobia (Burns, 1998; Clawson, 1991; Tobias, 1995) or the widespread phenomenon of people who say they never understood mathematics beyond routine and real world based arithmetic and geometric activities?

Another feature of children's mathematical gossip (that is, children's abstract play) is that they are explicitly aware that this is a game, that there are rules, and that the relationships are under their control. This feature sometimes disappears in a formal mathematics classroom. Mathematics is not an inevitable body of knowledge. Understanding it and doing it requires a consciousness of the 'rules' and the awareness that they are rules or conventions. Such awareness is particularly needed at the early stages where we often act as if there is nothing to be surprised about. The examples of fractions and multiplication are cases in point. In the real world multiplication is never commutative—it is only the abstraction of multiplication that is commutative. Often the numbers do not even represent the same kind of thing: 5 packets of biscuits at $3.80 each cost $19.00. Two of these numbers represent money, the other represents a counting number. We expect children to multiply in this situation, and to understand that multiplication is commutative. They need to know that this is the game.

Formal mathematics language is subtly different from everyday gossip. Think about the codes that develop amongst small communities of gossipers: phrases that take on special meanings so that an outsider might not get the full meaning of a statement. Mathematics has its own codes. The unexplained introduction of the codes of mathematics (that is, mathematics that is already formalised) may cause confusion. For example, at the elementary level, if a child is familiar with numbers describing "how many" and then, without apparent change of discourse, they hear numbers talked about as objects that can be manipulated independently of things being counted, it is no wonder that they become confused at what is going on.

Having a language that is in congruence with mathematics may be a two-edged sword educationally. On the one hand, it seems that there will be no cognitive disruption for students approaching mathematics. The way they have used numbers in everyday conversation will slowly evolve into the mathematical use of numbers, and no troubles will result. On the other hand, perhaps the way that concepts change without being noted or explained causes some of the problems experienced by young children? Is this the cause of widespread claims that people do not have a mathematical mind?

Reasons for concluding that such difficulties exist can be found in the history of mathematics. Rotman (1987, p. 8) records the difficulty mathematicians had with transforming the idea of nothing into a number. How can nothing be something? Nothing is the absence of something, even the absence of number—it cannot be a number itself. Are such difficulties replicated in some mathematics learners today, or does their common experience of zero appearing on a calculator overcome this particular language shift?

Mathematics as abstract gossip—the idea has led us to think that children should have more abstraction, not less, and that being aware of the rules of the game is an essential feature. What other implications can we draw for mathematics learning?

3. FROM 1 TO 100: PLAYING & EXPLORING

It is a curious feature of mathematics education that we expect and encourage exploratory and playful mathematical activity in very young children, and in advanced research mathematicians, but in between we sit students down to do exercises and listen to teachers or lecturers explain how it is. There are now secondary school classrooms where exploratory activity is encouraged, but as soon as the spectre of national examinations or international testing surveys looms close, mathematical activity reverts to closed exercises and transmission teaching.

I acknowledge some reasons for this: bureaucratic pressures to cover a defined syllabus; policy pressures to report in a particular way; pragmatic pressures to help students respond to the types of tests they will face; and teachers simply doing what they know best. However, from the point of view of learning to do mathematics well and effectively, and in order to experience the joy and beauty of mathematics, the removal of exploratory and playful opportunities from learning activity at secondary and tertiary levels is a very strange thing to do.

First of all, mathematical exploration and play is always possible, at any level. Within the environment of existing mathematics there are (have always been) educational resources full of wonderful open questions. However there is something more. We concluded above that mathematics could have been different. This conclusion does not just apply to research mathematics—it applies from the very first experiences with numbers and shapes, to beginning algebra, to practical and theoretical statistics, and to any branch of advanced mathematics. We can always do mathematical exploration outside the confines of NUC-mathematics. It is nearly always possible to change some basic assumption of mathematics, and to genuinely explore or play in a new environment. The Double Origin and Active Geometries discussed in Part I are examples.

Exploration and play are always possible: is it always a good idea to do it? One reason for playing with mathematics is because exploration is an interesting and efficient way to exhibit the nature of mathematics. Mathematics could have been (still can be) different. There are many untapped potential ideas that can be explored, and may even turn out to be useful or applicable. Having mathematical ability includes an attitude towards mathematics that assumptions can, and should, be questioned, and that changing (or creating new) assumptions leads to new ideas. Experiencing mathematics outside the normal conventions is the most direct and the most powerful way of developing these attitudes.

Another reason for mathematical play and exploration is that the ability to change mathematical contexts deliberately is part of the skill of doing mathematics. Not only is it necessary to be able to question mathematical assumptions, it is also necessary to step outside conceptual conventions. Many of these conventions are unrecognised and language-based, thus developing mathematical ability includes taking every opportunity to practice "thinking outside the square". Both changing assumptions within mathematics and conceptualising in original ways are useful habits at any level. We need to keep challenging established ideas at every stage in our learning.

Questioning and challenging assumptions are not just useful habits, they are vital skills for a mathematician. We should therefore be particularly concerned that exploratory and playful activity is largely absent in undergraduate mathematics—this is exactly where it should be most in evidence. In these classes we have collected the best young mathematical minds a society has. Why are they deprived of a mathematical activity that is both one of the most pleasurable and also one of the most important for their future work? The freedom of university study where new ideas and novel learning experiences abound is exactly the right environment for exploratory mathematics, but in mathematics at this level the approach is usually more closed and structured than ever before.

Not only is mathematical play and exploration necessary to understand the nature of mathematics, and necessary to be able to do mathematics, it is also necessary for the process of learning mathematics. Mathematics is created in the act of communicating human activity directed towards making sense of quantitative, relational, and spatial aspects of the world. Many argue that learning mathematics must reproduce the historical development of mathematics, the ontogenetic argument (Fauvel & van Maanen, 2001). If this is accepted then reproducing the exploratory experience is a vital component. However even if this argument is not accepted, there is still a need for these activities during learning. Mathematics is the abstract systematisation of experiences; it is a process as much as it is the result of a process. Learning mathematics cannot therefore just be learning about the completed system, it must also be learning the process—and there is no way to do that without undertaking the process. You cannot learn to drive a car from a book about driving.

Communication is a key element of the process. In order for communication to happen, not only do we need relevant experiences to communicate about, but we also need to have a reason to communicate, and, just as important in this case, a need to communicate formally. If the communication is about pre-formalised mathematics, then students will not learn the process of formalising for themselves.

In other words, they need original mathematical experiences to communicate. They need to be excited enough about them to both want to communicate them, and challenged enough to communicate about them precisely. Play and exploration are the first stage of this process.

4.   CREATING MATHEMATICS THROUGH TALKING

What does the conclusion that mathematics is created in the act of communicating mean for a learner? What are the special requirements of this form of communication?

I now need to abandon the metaphor of gossip. Mathematics is not gossip. Devlin only says that doing mathematics is in some ways like gossiping. Mainly, they are both about relationships. There are other ways in which mathematics is not at all like gossip. We can easily associate the adjective 'idle' to gossip, but formalised mathematics is far from idle. It is purposeful and directed. Gossip is rarely reproduced exactly: it is usually elaborated and embellished. Mathematics is deliberately created in such a way that it can be exactly repeated. Gossip thrives on ambiguity, suggestion, and nuance. Formalised mathematics, on the other hand, needs to be as precise and unambiguous as possible.

Learning mathematics is learning to communicate in particular ways about relationships. Part of learning the ability to formalise includes understanding the reason for formalising. Only through communicating back and forth can the need for precision of meaning become evident; and it is only by passing ideas through chains of communication that the need for reproducibility is experienced. Important ideas need to be communicated, and the more important they are, the more accurately and consistently they need to be communicated. Mathematical ideas must be systematised to be communicated, thus mathematics is created. This is why mathematics and language develop together.

In this process a mathematical world is created. Mathematics and language evolve together to create a world that is not the same as the real experiences from which it originated.

Take the example of 'membership'. The concept is a familiar one: we are members of a family, we are members of clubs, we hold membership cards to prove the relationship. Membership means that we are included, that we are part of a group

Here is a very simple problem involving family membership and its internal relations. Maria and Pedro Oliveras (who have since died) were married and their children were four sons: Carlos, Salvador, Garcia, and Juan. These sons are now the only members of the Oliveras family. One day, in a cafe, two members of the Oliveras family are standing at the bar. Are they brothers? Yes, they must be.

Now here is a mathematical problem that appears parallel, but is not because 'member' has a subtly different meaning. Let S be the set containing the four sons of the Oliveras family: Carlos, Salvador, Garcia and Juan. Mathematically this is written: S = {Carlos, Salvador, Garcia, Juan}. Thus each son is a member of the set S, we write Carlos $\in$ S. A mathematical question is: will two members of the set S always be brothers? The answer is "No". The reason is that, mathematically, the same member may be selected twice. That is "two members of the set S" includes the possibility of 'Juan' and 'Juan' being chosen. Juan is not his own brother.

This is confusing because we do not usually apply mathematical membership to people. The problem clarifies a little if I change set S to be the collection of *names* {Carlos, Salvador, Garcia, Juan}. Now if I ask two students to each choose a name, and ask whether the people corresponding to those names are brothers, it is more obvious that the two students could choose the same name.

It clarifies even further if I ask a parallel problem about numbers. Let B be the set {2, 4, 6, 8}. Let x and y be members of B and add $x + y$. Will the result always be a number between 5 and 15? No, because x and y can have the same value—they can both be the same member of the set B. For example they could both be 2. Now $2 + 2 = 4$ (which is less than 5). Or both could be 8, and $8 + 8 = 16$ (which is more than 15).

However this confusion of the meaning of membership and choosing x and y from a set is a common one. Ferrari (1999) did some research with a similar example using undergraduate mathematics students and found that even in a clearly mathematical context at an advanced level, the everyday meaning of membership interfered with their understanding of the mathematical question.

The mathematical world is not the same as the experiential world. The language changes, as do the concepts. Learning to be part of that world involves learning how it is created, and students need to experience the process of evolution. Being presented with the mathematical world, its concepts and language completely formed, will not help anyone to learn to be part of the evolution.

The formalisation of mathematical communication is not just a record of abstraction, it is also a way to enable abstraction to happen. Mathematics is not just gossip about abstraction, it is the formation of abstraction through communication. Once an abstract idea has been formalised it is available for further abstraction, an idea described by Piaget (1953), and developed for advanced mathematics as APOS theory by Dubinsky (1991). Once an idea has been formalised it is available again, layer upon layer of abstraction. For example, the joining of two collections is formalised as the arithmetical operation of addition; addition and subtraction and other operations are formalised as algebraic binary operations; binary operations and the objects they operate on are formalised as group theory; groups and their fundamental properties are formalised as topology; and so on and so on. This layering of abstraction is the real depth of mathematics, and is a clear example of the way mathematics and language must develop together. It also makes clear that learning mathematics must involve communicating about it.

The mathematical learner has one further task. A mathematician must also be able to talk about the process of abstraction in which they are engaged. There needs to be a meta-level language so that the mathematician can discuss the possibilities available for abstraction in any particular situation. The evidence from language shows that there are usually several directions we can take when making an abstraction. In order that a fuller range of choices is available, and that mathematical (rather than linguistic or experiential) decisions are made between them, the process needs to be articulated.

5.   SOME THOUGHTS ABOUT TEACHING MATHEMATICS

Before we consider the act of teaching, a few words on why we want to teach mathematics. If mathematics is not the highest expression of human thought (as Plato claimed), or even the science of what is clear by itself (as Jacobi suggested), then why should it be such a pervasive subject in our learning institutions? If it is, as I have claimed, a language dependent, context dependent, historically dependent view of the world, why is it endowed with such importance? If NUC-mathematics is not the only one possible, why does it have pre-eminence in curricula world-wide?

Mathematics is important for all the usual reasons: NUC-mathematics is the foundation of science and technology. It provides a suite of techniques and tools for business, engineering, medicine, architecture and design, navigation, astronomy, social science, and many other fields. It continues to enthral many great minds. Mathematics does turn out to be beautiful as well as unexpectedly effective (Wigner, 1960; Hamming, 1980). (Both its beauty and effectiveness are sourced in its connections with language and the evolution of abstract ways of thinking based on human experience). These reasons would suffice for mathematics' place in education. But another reason for teaching mathematics emerges from this book: mathematics helps us make personal sense of the world.

Now let us turn to teaching. What are the implications of the conclusions from language for those who facilitate, design, or control mathematics learning?

Note that all the ideas about learning detailed above have their parallels in teaching. If abstraction activities are needed at an early age, then teachers have a responsibility to provide them. Those responsible for young children can (and do) play many pre-mathematical games. They play with numbers in ways that do not involve counting; they draw plans of buildings and playgrounds, they draw maps of neighbourhoods, and they ask questions about the numbers, plans and maps. They tell stories that involve classification systems, and relations such as inclusion and size comparisons. These are all abstract experiences in quantity, space and relations.

Games can also be played with argumentation and logic. I once watched my brother at the zoo with my daughter (who was about four or five at the time). "There's a big animal," he said, looking at a rhinoceros, "it must be an elephant". "No," came the reply, "it's a rhinoceros". "But it's grey, and elephants are grey," he responded. "But it has a horn," she replied. "So have elephants—they have two ivory tusks and this has got two horns". "But elephants have trunks". "This elephant hasn't grown it yet". And so it went on, he forcing her to justify her statements, and countering them, and continuing the argument with other elephant characteristics (ears that flick, tail with a tuft of hair, mud on its legs, the noise it makes—of course the rhinoceros did not make any noise so she could not deny that he had got it wrong). It was not long before she turned the tables on him at another cage. The game of false or incomplete logic with ridiculous conclusions has been a family staple ever since.

I argue above that playing and exploring are vital parts of learning mathematics at all levels. Teachers, therefore, have an important role to provide opportunities, to model such activity, and to value it within their courses. This applies at university level, as much as it does in schools.

A teaching implication of the way mathematics is created through communication is the need to be explicit about the difference between everyday and formal mathematical talk. For a teacher not only does this mean that they should talk about this difference, for example, when discussing set membership, but they should also point out places where our everyday language is not quite adequate for mathematical discourse. An example arises from the unique feature of the Dhivehi language referred to in Part I.

In Dhivehi, we can refer to 'the book' by using the root word for book, *fot*. We can also refer to 'a book' meaning a particular but non-specified book, as in the sentence 'John was carrying a book when he fell into the water'. This sense of book is indicated by the suffix *–aku*, thus *fotaku*. There is a different word if we wish to refer to any book at all, as in the sentence 'John asked for a book to put on his papers so they would not blow away'. Here the book is a general book from the class of books. In Dhivehi this sense is indicated with a different suffix: *-ek*, thus *fotek*. The distinction is sometimes important in mathematics, but can be overlooked. An example occurs when drawing graphs of functions.

In the graph in Fig. 8-1 the variable x and the function $f(x)$ are each used in two ways, and these ways are different in the same way as the two different uses of 'book' described above. The 'x' in the expression $f(x) = 2x^2 + 1$ is any value of x at all—x is a variable. But the meaning of 'x' in the label P(x, $f(x)$) and the label on the horizontal axis is a particular, but unspecified, value of x. In this situation it is more correct to label the particular value as x_1, but often teachers do not do this, and slip between particular and general uses of a variable without thinking—to the confusion of their students.

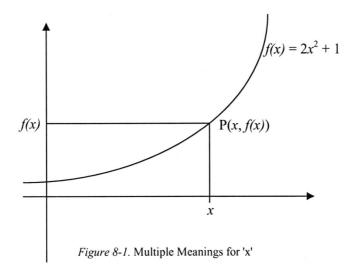

Figure 8-1. Multiple Meanings for 'x'

One more implication. The need to communicate, the need to play, the need to explore, and the need to learn about mathematics means that those charged with teaching the subject must themselves be more mathematically literate than ever before. If a teacher is to recognise, follow, and utilise the diverse mathematical thinking of children, then the more links, experiences, and applications on which to draw the better. They must know other ways of approaching the same idea; they must sense different directions in which the idea can be taken; they must be able to make use of cognitive conflicts that arise and new situations the children imagine.

In a world where the mathematical background of teachers is a cause for concern in many countries, an increasing mathematical demand on teachers may not be welcome—but it cannot be ignored.

6.   NOTES ON ASSESSMENT

First, let us remember that all the learning activities described above are linked to assessment. They are linked both because assessment is part of the pedagogical process, and they are linked because most formal institutionalised learning has a summative assessment requirement.

Assessment can be a way in which aspects of the pedagogical process are valued. Mathematics is a gatekeeper well beyond its real status, thus those parts of mathematics that are measured become part of the process for deciding on vocational and educational opportunities. Hence exactly those parts of mathematics receive focus and teacher input. So much is commonly understood.

The problem is, that if the conclusions from language are true, then what is needed for successful mathematical activity is exceedingly difficult—if not impossible—to measure. How do you evaluate creating a base of abstract experiences? By their definition, experiences are many and varied, and you cannot know in advance which ones will be used in later, formal, mathematical, abstraction activities. How are playing and creativity to be measured? The very act of attempting to measure them will kill them as play or as creativity. How is communicative mathematising to be measured? This latter might be partially possible with one-on-one interviews and recording group activities, but is hardly practicable as a routine for all students. The Numeracy Programme developed in New Zealand in 2002 onwards does just this: teachers are helped to evaluate each child's position on a framework of mathematical development through interviews. Irrespective of possible benefits, the practicality of such interviews as a regular part of the mathematics classroom leaves little time for other types of teacher/student interaction.

We are left on the horns of a dilemma. Either these vital features of mathematics education are not assessed and will not be valued (probably leading to being neglected by teachers and students alike), or they are assessed badly at a high cost in terms of time, teacher resources, and impact on the activity itself.

I am convinced that we need to wrestle with the first of these horns, not because of the resource cost of the second (if it is important enough, resources are usually found), but because assessment will ultimately kill these vital activities.

This means that having a variety of abstraction experiences, indulging in mathematical creativity and play, and communicating mathematically all need to be given high value in some way other than by assessment. This can be done by individual teachers—but such a solution is unlikely to be universally adopted. Another strategy is to highlight this activity amongst mathematical practitioners (not just mathematicians, but also system analysts, designers, engineers, information scientists, and so on).

The conclusions of this book lead us to downplay assessment for further reasons. Two of the conclusions about mathematics are, first, that mathematics is in continual formation, and second that mathematics is open in the sense that it could have been otherwise. The first means that it is never finished, the second means that there is always another way of perceiving, conceiving, or receiving mathematical ideas.

Given these parameters, assessment of learning mathematics as a whole is impossible. Assessment needs to be against something, a framework, a standard, another performance. But if mathematical learning is forever unfinished, and if it proceeds along any of a myriad of pathways, then there is no way of creating the basis for judgement. Any assessment that takes place compromises the nature of mathematics.

A final note on assessment concerns the conclusion that mathematics and language develop together: it is not possible to have mathematics without language.

A research project aimed at investigating the situation of senior secondary students with Mandarin as their first language learning mathematics in English involved giving them the same test in English and Mandarin (Neville-Barton & Barton, 2004). These students had done all their education in China except for the last few months. Their English proficiency was not high. Not surprisingly, the performance was better in Mandarin, but a large variation emerged between questions. Students performed the questions with technical vocabulary, complex syntax, or an unfamiliar context much better in the Mandarin version. One question, however, was done better in the English version. This was a question involving the concept of *gradient*.

The teachers reported that this concept was the only one in the test which had been taught for the first time in English, and that the term does not translate easily into Mandarin. This may explain the result, but it begs the question: what is the true mathematical understanding of these students? If some parts of mathematics are understood in English, and others in Mandarin, then what sort of test can evaluate mathematics? A bilingual test is not the answer, because even within one language there are many ways of expressing an idea, and many different associations for what might appear to be the same mathematical process—take, for example, the concepts of anti-differentiation and integration.

The chimera of mathematical ability, let alone the measurement of this ability, disappears into the mists of language, no matter how precise we think we are.

Chapter 9

MULTILINGUAL AND INDIGENOUS MATHEMATICS EDUCATION

Abstract: The conclusions in the previous chapter are specifically considered in relation to multilingual environments for learning mathematics, and for the education of indigenous peoples. It is argued that linguistic richness of these situations, and the multiple mathematical perspectives they bring to the classroom are resources that can be effectively utilised by teachers.

Keywords: multilingual mathematics, bilingual mathematics, indigenous mathematics education

This chapter is not a comprehensive look at the many sensitive, important, and controversial issues that surround mathematics education in multilingual classrooms or in indigenous contexts. Rather it is a commentary on what the conclusions reached in this book have to say on these matters.

Educators have often approached mathematics education in multilingual environments as a problematic situation: how can all the students understand; how can mathematical communication take place; why are minority students underachieving? Considerable research has addressed these issues (for example, *Educational Studies in Mathematics: Special Issue on Multilingual Issues in Mathematical Classrooms, 64*(2)), describing what goes on in multilingual mathematics classrooms (for example, Setati & Adler, 2001), investigating the underlying causes (for example, Moschkovich, 2002), studying teaching practices (for example, Adler, 2001), reporting on intervention programmes, and examining mathematics cognition in different languages (for example, Miura, Okamoto, Kim, Chang, Steere, & Fayol, M., 1994).

Our conclusions about mathematics from language evidence point to another perspective on multilingual classrooms: that of a fertile environment that could be the source of some highly creative and effective mathematics teaching and learning, as well as places that might produce innovative mathematicians.

1.   UNTOLD RICHES

Multilingual classrooms are linguistically rich—not only will more than one language be represented, but also the languages are often structurally diverse and well-resourced. That is to say that many students will have wide linguistic resources, for example, grandparents who carry the knowledge of elders, or other family members who speak other languages. The resource can usually be tapped. What is more, in these environments, multilingualism is the norm: students are adept at swapping between languages, seeing correspondences and differences, and using language creatively as they communicate with speakers of other languages.

These students know that languages do not interfere with each other, neither in their learning, nor in their use. If the students are young, they learned these languages naturally and easily from their environment.

Our conclusions about mathematics and language also imply a mathematical richness in multilingual classrooms. Each language carries parallel, but often different, conceptions of quantity, space and relationships. These mathematical worlds will be natural to the students, and, (depending on their fluency in various languages), they will be adept at moving between them, using whichever world is appropriate to best represent the idea they are trying to develop. Students will also be able to compare these different aspects of mathematics, and are likely to be interested in discussing them. My experience in such environments is that students are keen to talk about different vocabulary and usage.

When the Maori language was being developed for immersion teaching of mathematics, the students in my colleagues' class took to the challenges enthusiastically and creatively—for example, I leave the reader to make the connections between their suggestions for the terms *waewaekuri* (dogleg) for a cubic curve, and *mangopare* (hammerhead shark) for a rectangular hyperbola.

Inferring from language, where there is an additive effect if two (or more) languages are understood above "threshold" levels (Cummins, 1986), it is reasonable to conclude that having more than one point of view from which to approach mathematising will result in better understanding, more creative constructions, and more opportunities to abstract.

The mathematical potential of a multilingual student will increase the more deeply embedded that person becomes in the mathematics of all his or her languages. There is a tendency to aim for mathematics in English because that is the international medium of communication in the subject, and research mathematicians with non-English first languages increasingly research, discuss, and teach their subject in English. But we can conclude that mathematical advantages will result from maintaining and practising mathematical fluency in as many languages as possible.

Returning to the multilingual classroom, the issue for the teacher is how to make use of this potential. We must acknowledge that lower proficiency in one or more of their languages dulls the student's richness, but does not remove it. The trick is to see the situation as rich. I have experienced a classroom where the teacher perceived his mathematics class as having serious language problems: but 90% of the students spoke at least two languages fluently, and over 60% spoke three. They just did not speak English very well, and English was the only language he could use. In this situation it is not the students who have language problems—it is the teacher! In order to progress, it is preferable not to identify language as the problem: the problem is communication, and it belongs to everyone.

Once the issue is rephrased in this way, then it can be seen that monolingualising the mathematics teaching and learning into English is unlikely to be a good strategy, even if the ultimate aim is for everyone to be able to do mathematics in English (as is often claimed).

If the problem is communication, then the obvious strategy is to use all the resources at hand, not to restrict them. In the above case, for example, the monolingual teacher might use students' peers to generate first-language mathematics discussions, or start to learn, and use, some mathematical terms from other languages. The family resources could be invoked, and texts in other languages provided. The opportunities to increase English understanding would increase, not decrease, with such activity. No adverse interference is likely to occur.

However there is more than this. Language diversity itself also offers some resources for new teaching and learning techniques.

Using students' own resources is always an effective motivator, especially in cases where students know more than the teacher. Hence pedagogies that involve the language diversity of the class are likely to be effective. This is not just a technique for young students. Imagine an English-language university tutorial where the professor asks a student to work through a problem using their own language, one that is not spoken by others in the class. If all were willing to engage, comprehending the student's work would be an interesting exercise that would focus attention on justifications (through their incomprehensibility), symbolisations (through the reliance on them as communication), and creative thinking (as students tried to fill in for themselves what they did not understand).

Making mathematics learning more explicitly parallel to language learning provides new and effective ways of presenting material for all students. Language learning techniques such as split information tasks have been used successfully in monolingual as well as multilingual situations. Much work has already been done in these areas, and a quick web-search will find many resources at any level.

2.   MATHEMATICAL DISCOURSE

A particular source of linguistic richness in the mathematics classroom is the variety of mathematical discourse.

The idea that mathematical language is different from everyday language has not been a large part of this book, although it is an important aspect of mathematics and language. The linguist Halliday (1975) first discussed mathematical discourse, and many articles since have described the differences between mathematical and general discourse in English (for example, Dale & Cuevas, 1987; Esty, 1992). For example, quite apart from the appearance of symbols, written mathematics is much more conceptually dense, there are many more logical connectives, and adjectives and prepositions are much more important than in written English. To illustrate the last point, consider the difference between:

The cost was reduced by $10	means...	Cost - $10 = New price
The cost was reduced to $10	means...	Cost – Reduction = $10
The cost was reduced from $10	means...	$10 – Reduction = New price
The cost was reduced $10	means...	Cost - $10 = New price

I often wonder how students who are learners of English cope in a classroom when a teacher makes statements such as these. Hearing prepositions in spoken English is very difficult—try getting someone to read the sentences above, and listen for the prepositions.

While mathematical discourse has most likely developed in response to a need for exactness of language in mathematics, many expressions are, in English, far from unambiguous. For example, to stay with prepositions, the words *into* and *by* can each be used on their own to indicate multiplication or division:

$15 \div 2$ and 15×2 are both expressed as "fifteen by two" depending on the country you are in and the context of the calculation.

$5{\overline{)16}}$ is described as "five *into* sixteen", but the algebraic expression $2(a + b)$ is also read as "two *into* a plus b".

There are big differences between mathematical discourse in different languages: the way proportion is expressed; the way an inference is made; the way existence or universality is indicated. Again, much has been written in this area (for example, for Mandarin, see Galligan, 2001), and the educational implications of these observations are significant, particularly for multilingual classrooms. Teachers may see such differences as cause for confusion, but the way in which mathematical discourse in different languages fits (or does not fit) with the symbolised expression of the statement is a rich source of mathematical discussion. Using language richness to highlight spoken/symbolised relationships is an effective strategy to alert students to areas (like proportion, inference, or quantifiers) that are common sources of misunderstanding.

Those people who have tried to write equivalent mathematics questions in different languages for Olympiad competitions or for international comparative studies will know that some mathematical problems are easier when expressed in one language compared with another. Can such differences be used educationally? Certainly. The New Zealand national mathematics curriculum suggests that young children should be taught to count in Maori or another clearly base-ten language, rather than English. The idiosyncratic names for 11 and 12, and the reversal of tens and digits in naming the teens does not help the early development of base ten counting or writing figures correctly.

A final note about mathematical discourse. Mathematics embodies a world that is related to the language spoken. That world is fundamental in the sense that it captures how we come to comprehend vital aspects of our experience: our idea of quantity, our conception of space, and the ways that we relate things to each other. Mathematics, therefore, is a useful environment for learning about other cultural views. In particular, it might be a useful environment for learning another language.

This idea has been discussed in the context of Maori immersion education (Fairhall, 1993) where one of the aims is the rejuvenation of the Maori language. And that is a good point at which to transfer our attention to indigenous peoples' mathematics education.

3.   MATHEMATICS EDUCATION FOR INDIGENOUS PEOPLES

Socio-political context is everything. In 1994 I visited South Africa, then newly emerged under Mandela as a unified, apartheid-free nation. I was still involved with the last stages of the Maori vocabulary development project with which this book began, and had recently come from teaching mathematics in Maori at a bilingual unit in an inner-city high school.

At the (then) University of Durban-Westville, I was privileged to visit some teachers from Zululand who were on an in-service mathematics course. At the end of their session we chatted informally. Did they use SiZulu in their mathematics classrooms, I wanted to know? An embarrassed silence, glances at each other and around the room. "Yes", one finally admitted quietly, "but we are not supposed to". "But you are all first language Zulu speakers?" "Yes." "And your students are all first-language Zulu speakers?" "Yes." "And they have some difficulty with English?" "Yes." It emerged that they were not permitted to use SiZulu at all, and that their principal would go around listening at the door to check that they did not use it—hence their reluctance to admit it. This school policy was justified by arguments about the ultimate learning goal being mathematics in English and the benefits of fluency in both a world language and a home language, and the educational research that showed that immersion in the target language was the best strategy.

This was curious for me. In New Zealand at that time the existence of fluent Maori-speaking teachers and students would have been welcomed by any school, and the opportunity taken to establish Maori language instruction with a lot of resources made available. Every teacher in every class in New Zealand was being encouraged to use whatever Maori vocabulary they could in appropriate places in their lesson. This behaviour was justified by arguments about the ultimate learning goal being mathematics in English and the benefits of fluency in both a world language and a home language, and by the educational research that showed that immersion in the target language was the best strategy.

Yes, the same justification for two opposing educational policies. The explanation is not hard to find. New Zealand was going through a Maori cultural renaissance with a lot of pride being taken in our national language and heritage. South Africa, on the other hand, was newly emerged from an oppressive political regime in which one of the instruments of oppression was a law requiring education in the home language. In South Africa I was in quite a sensitive situation as a white male supporting home language instruction! In education, socio-political context is everything.

The practical reality is that every indigenous peoples' context is different: different with respect to their knowledge and use of languages; different with respect to their political situation in their own country; different with respect to their aims for education; different with respect to their access to resources; and more. However, some features of the many indigenous contexts are generally similar. The similarities make it possible to use our conclusions to make some suggestions.

Most indigenous peoples are relatively culturally homogenous and have some identity, often including location, within the wider society of the country (or countries) in which they live. In many cases the children are deeply immersed in their indigenous cultural world. Their home language and world-view are predominant in their lives, although they are subordinate in the wider, or national, community. We can assume, therefore, that an indigenous community is the environment where a mathematical world different from NUC-mathematics will be most strongly felt.

Educationally, indigenous peoples are likely to have some communal aims for education that are different from those for wider society. However, in most such societies of my experience, an understanding of NUC-mathematics and a world-language such as English are included as desired outcomes, representing access to communication, further educational opportunities, employment, and development.

How do we introduce children who have grown up in one world-view to a different world-view? What are useful teaching approaches for groups of children speaking a language less consonant with NUC-mathematics and with deeply embedded concepts of quantity, relationships and space at odds with the concepts of NUC-mathematics?

One implication of what has gone before has already emerged in our discussion of the multi-lingual classroom. As a practical matter, in a linguistic environment of many speakers of one language who are at a similar stage of development with respect to English (or another world language), using the fluent language to assist the transition between worlds and development of new ideas is strongly indicated. A teacher with the same first-language as the children is in an especially privileged position to utilise language resources.

But the mistake often made in mathematics classrooms is that teachers assume that the NUC-mathematics of the target curriculum is unproblematic as a subject. Understanding NUC-mathematics is not the same as understanding the nature of mathematics. Proficiency in the subject can lead to access, and is therefore a sensible educational aspiration, But knowing why mathematics performs this function, understanding its role in the lives of individuals or society, and comprehending the nature of the subject, is just as vital as an educational goal. My experience tells me that these three aspects of mathematics are not understood in most educational environments.

The problem is that, especially in indigenous peoples' education, not paying attention to the nature of mathematics may have devastating educational effects. The relative alienation of indigenous children to mathematics (and science) can be explained at least partially because they are less likely to accept mathematics as relevant to their lives. If I do not know what I'm supposed to be learning, or why, then I am not likely to be interested in learning it. And if this thing I'm supposed to be learning is regarded as very important in the world, and if I'm failing, then yes, I'll be even more alienated.

Because we do not teach mathematics as culturally dependent, and because we do not acknowledge that NUC-mathematics may potentially conflict with deeply-held concepts and the means of

expressing them, we generate alienation and thereby under-achieve-
ment by communities of indigenous children. Individual children or
communities often interpret reduced success as personal or group
failure rather than systemic failure. Furthermore, because mathematics
is related to measures of intelligence, educational ability, and social
selection mechanisms, reduced success in mathematics impacts on
self-esteem, future opportunities, and class divisions based on culture.
Mathematics does this more strongly than other subjects.

What might educationalists and teachers do to help? One suggestion seems ridiculous in its simplicity, but I believe is both neglected
and vital. We must explain what mathematics is—and we must do
it in a way that children understand. We must not assume that
mathematics is self-explanatory in its purpose or in its relation to
society.

This injunction applies to all mathematics learning situations, not
just indigenous ones. However, the consequence of not taking account
of mathematics' purpose and role is potentially much more disabling
in those communities that are embedded in world-views and
languages at odds with NUC-mathematics.

What is the purpose and role of mathematics? The purpose is
implied in my alternative description of mathematics: it is a system
created by humans to help them understand their experiences of
quantity, relationships, and space. Mathematics is an abstraction contained within language and symbols that, once devised, can be both
developed of itself or manipulated and used in relation to the world
and ourselves in it.

The role of mathematics is primarily to help us understand and act
within our world. It is a tool to "construct our future" as D'Ambrosio
explains (in a speech reported in Barton, Domite, & Poisard, 2006,
p. 25):

> Individuals create instruments (such as mathematics) to enhance the
> possibility of survival and the transcendence of time and space. In this
> search, people attempt to explain the phenomena they encounter. These
> models and explanations are an attempt to know (and control) the future.

D'Ambrosio offers ethnomathematics as a proposal that will
ultimately (Barton, Domite, & Poisard, 2006, p. 25):

> ...[create] a civilisation with dignity for all, free of inequity, arrogance,
> and bigotry. ... The pedagogical aims are to promote creativity in helping

people reach their mathematical potential, and citizenship, by transmitting human values and responsibility within society.

In this view, mathematics is much more that a system of equations to be studied for the construction of bridges or business. It is part of the essence of how we are to live as human beings.

How can teachers in indigenous communities communicate the role and purpose of mathematics? Through the QRS systems of the indigenous culture, of course. By fully understanding those systems with which you are familiar, the awareness of other systems (and an interest in them) can be better generated.

The children in indigenous cultures have the means to understand better than other children the nature and role of QRS systems, since they will have some knowledge of more than one culturally developed system. (I note that all children do have experience of alternative QRS systems, often generated in the youth subculture to which they belong, but that culturally developed systems are likely to be more comprehensive, more deeply embedded in language, and more widely known).

There are at least two programmes that I am aware of where this kind of thinking is driving a mathematics education programme, one in Fairbanks Alaska where a team including Jerry Lipka, Evelyn Yanez, and Dora Andrew-Ihrke have for many years been incorporating Yup'ik systems into their mathematics education (Lipka, Yanez, & Andrew-Ihrke, 2006). They have evidence that their programme enhances the conventional mathematics performance of Yup'ik students. In The Maldives, Shehenaz Adam (2004) trialled a unit of work based on the same principles, and developed a theoretical framework on which some of the ideas above are based.

The programmes that consider indigenous QRS systems as systems in themselves are very different from the unintegrated or casual use of cultural materials in a NUC-mathematics classroom. Such use may have small-scale pedagogical or motivational value for students, although my own experience leads me to be very cautious about taking cultural materials out of context.

Note that the incorporation of an understanding of indigenous QRS-systems into a mathematics programme is being justified here for its efficacy in promoting the ultimate aim of understanding NUC-mathematics, albeit in a humanistic way. The success of such an approach is to be partially judged on successful learning of

NUC-mathematics, and partially on the ultimate use and values that students gain from mathematics in general.

Finally let us return to a key conclusion of this book: mathematics and language develop together. Hence, indigenous students learning NUC-mathematics will be partially learning mathematical language in a way that those whose first language is English will not. It is even more important, therefore, that attention is paid to mathematical communication as a source of mathematics learning. And that is as good a sum-up statement as I can find.

END WORDS

Let us summarise. First the conclusions predominantly related to mathematics.

M1 Mathematics and language develop together. Historically this has been so, each of these two areas of human activity affect the other.

M2 There are choices that get made in the origins and development of mathematics. Mathematics could be different. A corollary of this is that there are still many undeveloped mathematical ideas.

M3 Mathematics is created by communicating, that is, mathematics is created in the act of communication about the QRS aspects of our world. A corollary of this is that mathematics is both enabled and restricted by the conventions of communication.

M4 Mathematics arises after, not before, human activity, in response to human thinking about quantity, relationships, and space within particular socio-cultural environments. Thus the factors determining the choices made in the development of mathematics are primarily social and cultural.

M5 Languages contain their own mathematical worlds. These worlds represent systems of meaning concerned with quantity, relationships, or space.

I make three further conclusions that relate to mathematical language.

L1 Mathematical language development is in the direction of more similarity, that is, all languages are evolving to express QRS ideas in ways that are more and more the same.

L2 Mathematical language (not just mathematics) evolves from the physical and social environment.

L3 Mathematical language is more consonant with some languages, and less consonant with others.

And finally four conclusions related to mathematics education.

E1   The key to understanding mathematics is to have a wide range of abstracting experiences from the everyday world on which to draw.

E2   Learning mathematics, and doing mathematics, involves talking mathematics: the more we talk mathematics, the better we will learn it and do it.

E3   Multilingual classrooms are potentially fertile mathematical learning environments because of their linguistic richness.

E4   Indigenous peoples can access better understanding of the nature and structures of mathematics through a thorough understanding of the nature and role of their own QRS systems.

REFERENCES

Abelson, H. & diSessa, A. (1980). *Turtle Geometry: The Computer as a Medium for Exploring Mathematics*. Massachusetts: MIT Press.

Académie Tahitienne, (1986). *La Grammaire de la Langue Tahitienne*. Papeete, Tahiti: Académie Tahitienne.

Adam, S. (2004). Ethnomathematics in the Maldivian Curriculum: Trialling an Implementation. Unpublished Doctoral Thesis. The University of Auckland.

Adler, J. (2001). *Teaching Mathematics in Multilingual Classrooms*, Dordrecht, Kluwer.

Akimichi, T. (1985). Navigational Knowledge of the Yetak System and the Allocation at Sea on Satawal, Central Caroline Islands. *Bulletin of the National Museum of Ethnology (Osaka) 10*(4), 931–957.

Appel, K. & Haken, W. (1997). Every planar map is four colorable. Part 1. Discharging. *Illinois Journal of Mathematics 21*, 429–490.

Appel, K., Haken, W., & Koch, J. (1977). Every planar map is four colorable. Part II. Reducibility, *Illinois Journal of Mathematics 21*, 491–567.

Ascher, M. (1991). *Ethnomathematics: A Multicultural View of Mathematical Ideas*. Pacific Grove, CA: Brooks/Cole Publishing Company

Ascher, M. (2002). The Kolam Tradition. *American Scientist, 90*, 57–63.

Aspin, C. (1995). Mathematics Achievement in a Kura Kaupapa Maori. In Te Puni Kokiri, *Proceedings of the National Association of Maori Mathematics Science And Technology Inaugural Conference*, p. 93–4, Wellington: Te Puni Kokiri.

Aristotle. *Physics VI*(9), 239b5.

Bagrow, L. (1985) *The History of Cartography*.

Barton, B. (1996). *Ethnomathematics: Exploring Cultural Diversity in Mathematics*. Unpublished Phd, University of Auckland, Auckland.

Barton, B., Fairhall, U., & Trinick, T. (1995a). Whakatupu Reo Tatai: History of the Development of Maori Mathematics Vocabulary, *SAMEpapers 1995*, p. 144–160.

Barton, B., Fairhall, U., & Trinick, T. (1995b). He Korero Kupu Tatai: Word Stories in Maori Mathematics Vocabulary Development. In B. Barton & U. Fairhall (Eds.) *Mathematics In Maori Education*, 9–13, Unpublished collection of papers available from the Mathematics Education Unit, Department of Mathematics, University of Auckland, New Zealand.

Barton, B., Fairhall, U., & Trinick, T. (1998). Tikanga Reo Tatai: Issues in the Development of a Maori Mathematics Register, *For The Learning of Mathematics, 18*(1), 3–9.

Barton, B., Lichtenberk, F., & Reilly, I. (2005). The Language of Topology: A Turkish Case Study. Applied General Topology, *6*(2), 107–117. http://at.yorku.ca/i/a/a/k/24.htm.

Barton, B. & Reilly, I. (1999). Topological Concepts and Language: A Report of Research in Progress. Notices of the South African Mathematical Society, *30*(2), 110–119.

Barton, B., Domite, M., & Poisard, C. (2006). Cultural Connections and Mathematical Manipulations. *For The Learning of Mathematics, 26*(2), 22–26.

Baude, P. (2003). Personal communication from the ex–French Ambassador to the Pacific.

Berggren, J. L. (1986). *Episodes in the Mathematics of Medieval Islam*. Frankfurt: Springer–Verlag.

Berggren, J. L. (1990). Proof, Pedagogy, and the Practice of Mathematics in Medieval Islam. In *Interchange 21*(1) 36–48.

Berger, J. O. (1980). *Statistical Decision Theory: Foundations, Concepts, and Methods*. New York: Springer–Verlag, Springer Series in Statistics.

Biggs, B. (1969). *Let's Learn Maori: A Guide to the Study of the Maori Language*. Wellington; A.H. & A.W. Reed.

Bishop, A. J. (1988). *Mathematical Enculturation: A Cultural Perspective on Mathematics Education*. Dordrecht: Kluwer Academic Publishers.

Bishop, A. J. (1990). Western Mathematics: the Secret Weapon of Cultural Imperialism, in *Race & Class, 32*(2) 51–65.

Bloor, D. (1973). Wittgenstein and Mannheim on the Sociology of Mathematics. In *Studies in History and Philosophy of Science, 4*(2), 173–191.

Bloor, D (1976). *Knowledge and Social Imagery*, London: Routledge & Kegan Paul (Page references are to the Second Edition, Chicago: University of Chicago Press (1991)).

Bloor, D. (1978). Polyhedra and the Abominations of Leviticus. In *The British Journal for the History of Science, 11*(39), 245–77.

Bloor, D (1983). *Wittgenstein. A Social Theory of Knowledge*, London: MacMillan Press.

Bloor, D. (1994). What Can the Sociologist of Knowledge Say About 2 + 2 = 4?. In P. Ernest (ed) *Mathematics, Education and Philosophy: An International Perspective*, p. 21–32. London: The Falmer Press

Borwein, J. (1999). The Doing of Mathematics in the Presence of Technology. Session on Electronic Information and Communication, Joint Australian–American Mathematical Society Meetings, Melbourne, July 12–15, 1999.

Burling, R. (1965). How To Choose a Burmese Number Classifier. In M. E. Spiro (ed) *Context and Meaning in Cultural Anthropology*, p. 243–264. New York:

Burns, M. (1998): *Math: Facing an American Phobia*. Maths Solutions Publications.

Butterworth, B. (1999). *The Mathematical Brain*. Basingstoke, UK: Macmillan.

Chomsky, N. (1998). *On Language*. New York: The New Press.

Clawson, C. (1991). *Conquering Math Phobia: A Painless Primer*. New York: John Wiley & Sons.

Cohen, B. (1984). Florence Nightingale. In *Scientific American*, 1984, 98–107.

Collinder, P. (1954). *A History of Marine Navigation*, London: Batsford.

Contreras, L., Morales, J., & Ramirez, J. (Eds.) (1998). *Proceedings of the First International Congress on Ethnomathematics (ICEM1)*, CD Rom, Universidad de Granada, Granada, Spain.

Corbey, R. & Leerssen, J. (Eds.) (1991). *Alterity, Identity, Image. Selves and Others in Society and Scholarship*. Amsterdam Series on Cultural identity 1. Amsterdam–Atlanta, GA: Rodopi.

Cummins, J. (1986). *Bilingualism in Education: Aspects of Theory, Research and Practice*. London: Longman.

Dale, T. & Cuevas, G. (1987). Integrating Language and Mathematics Learning. In J. Crandall (ed) *ESL Through Content–Area Instruction*, 9–52, Englewood Cliffs, NJ: Prentice Hall Regents.

David, F. (1962). *Games, Gods, & Gambling*. London: Griffin.

Davis, P. J. (1993). Applied Mathematics As Social Contract. In S. Restivo, J. P. van Bendegem & R. Fischer (eds) *Math Worlds: Philosophical and Social Studies of Mathematics and Mathematics Education*, New York: State University of New York Press.

Davis, P. J. & Hersh, R. (1981). *The Mathematical Experience*. Boston: Birkhäuser.

Davis, P. J. & Hersh, R. (1986). *Descartes' Dream: The World According to Mathematics*. San Diego: Harcourt Brace Jovanich.

Dehaene, S. (1997). *The Number Sense: How Mind Creates Mathematics*. Oxford, UK: Oxford University Press.

Denny, P. (1986). Cultural Ecology of Mathematics: Ojibway and Inuit Hunters. In M. P. Closs (ed) *Native American Mathematics*, p. 129–180. Austin: University of Texas Press.

Devlin, K. (2001). *The Maths Gene: Why everyone has it, but most people don't use it*. London: Phoenix.

Dubinsky, E. (1991). Reflective abstraction in advanced mathematical thinking. In D. Tall (Ed.), *Advanced Mathematical Thinking*, p. 95–126. Dordrecht: Kluwer Academic Publishers.

Epstein, D. & Levy, S. (1995). Experimentation and Proof in Mathematics. In *Notices of the American Mathematics Society, 42*(6), 670–674.

Esty, W. (1992). Language Concepts of Mathematics. *Focus on Learning Problems in Mathematics, 14*(4), 31–54.

Eves, H. (1969). The History of Geometry: An Overview. In *Historical Topics for the Mathematics Classroom: 31st Yearbook of NCTM*, p. 165–191. Washington: National Council of Teachers of Mathematics.

Fairhall, U. (1993). Mathematics as a Vehicle for the Acquisition of Maori, *SAMEpapers 1993*, p. 116–123.

Fang, J. & Takayama, K (1975). *Sociology of Mathematics and Mathematicians. A Prolegomenon*. Hauppauge, N.Y.: Paideia Press.

Fauvel, J. & van Maanen, J. (Eds.) (2001). *History in Mathematics Education: The ICMI Study*. Dordrecht: Kluwer Academic Publishers.

Ferrari, P. (1999). Cooperative principles and Linguistic Obstacles in Advanced Mathematics Learning. In I. Schwank (Ed.), *Proceedings of the First Conference of the European Society for Research in Mathematics Education*, Vol. II., Norderstedt, Germany: Libri.

Galligan, L. (2001). Possible Effects of English–Chinese Language Differences on the Processing of Mathematical Text: A Review, *Mathematics Education Research Journal, 13*(2), 112–132.

Gardner, M. (1966). *New Mathematical Diversions: More Puzzles, Problems, Games, and Other Mathematical Diversions*. New York: Simon & Schuster.

Gay, J. & Cole, M. (1967). *The New Mathematics and an Old Culture: A Study of Learning among the Kpelle of Nigeria*. New York: Holt, Rinehart & Winston.

Gillies, D. (Ed.) (1992). *Revolutions in Mathematics*. Oxford: Clarendon Press.

Gladwin, T. (1970). *East is a Big Bird: Navigation and Logic on Puluwat Atoll*. Cambridge, MA: Harvard University Press.

Gunn, M. 1970. *Etak and Other Concepts Underlying Carolinian Navigation*. M.A. thesis in Anthropology, University of Otago.

Hacking, I. (1975). *The Emergence of Probability: A Philosophical Study of Early Ideas About Probability, Induction and Statistical Inference*. Cambridge: Cambridge University Press.

Halliday, M. (1975). Some Aspects of Sociolinguistics. In E. Jacobsen (ed) *Interactions Between Language and Mathematical Education: UNESCO Report No. ED–74/CONF–808*, 64–73, Paris: UNESCO. Reprinted 1978 as Sociolinguistic Aspects of Mathematical Education, in M. Halliday, *Language as Social Semiotic*, p. 194–204, London: Edward Arnold.

Hamming, R. W. (1980). The Unreasonable Effectiveness of Mathematics in the Natural Sciences. *American Mathematical Monthly, 87*(2).

Hardy, G. H. (1941). *A Mathematician's Apology*. Cambridge: Cambridge University Press.

Hardy, G. (1978). *Ramanujan: Twelve Lectures on Subjects Suggested by his Life and Work.* (3rd Edition). New York: Chelsea Publishing Co.

Harlow, R. (2001). *A Maori Reference Grammar.* Auckland: Longman.

Harris, P. (1991). *Mathematics in a Cultural Context.* Geelong: Deakin University.

Hess, H. (2002). *The Glass Bead Game: (Magister Ludi) A Novel.* New York: Picador.

Heyerdahl, T. (1958). *Kon–Tiki: Across the Pacific by Raft.* New York: Simon & Schuster.

Hill, D. (1997). Finding Your Way in Longgu: Geographical Reference in a Solomon Islands Language. In G. Senft (Ed.), *Referring to Space: Studies in Austronesian and Papuan Languages,* p. 101–126. Oxford: Clarendon Press.

Hofstadter, D. R. (1979). *Godel, Escher, Bach: The Eternal Golden Braid.* New York: Basic Books.

Hutchins, E. (1983) Understanding Micronesian Navigation. In Gentner & Stevens (Eds.), *Mental Models.* Hillsdale NJ: Lawrence Erlbaum Associates.

Irwin, G. (1992). *The Prehistoric Exploration and Colonisation of the Pacific,* Cambridge, NY: Cambridge University Press.

Joseph, G. G. (1992). *The Crest of the Peacock: Non–European Roots of Mathematics.* London: Penguin.

Joseph, G. G. (1994). Different Ways of Knowing: Contrasting Styles of Argument in Indian and Greek Mathematical Traditions. In P. Ernest (Ed.) *Mathematics, Education and Philosophy: An International Perspective,* London: The Falmer Press.

Kaplan, A. (1960). Sociology Learns the Language of Mathematics. In J. R. Newman (Ed.) The World of Mathematics Vol II, p. 1294–313. London: George, Allen & Unwin Ltd.

Khare, H. C. (Ed.) (1988). *Proceedings of the National Workshop on Vedic Mathematics, 25–28 March,* University of Rajastan, Jaipur. Dehli: Motilal Banarsidass Publishers.

Klein, J. (1968). *Greek Mathematical Thought and the Origin of Algebra.* Cambridge, MA: MIT Press.

Kline, M. (1973). *Why Johnny Can't Add: The Failure of the New Math.* New York: St Martin's Press.

Kline, M. (1980). *Mathematics: The Loss of Certainty.* Oxford: Oxford University Press.

Klir, G., St. Clair, U., & Bo Yuan (1997). *Fuzzy Set Theory: Foundations and Applications.* Englewood Cliffs, NJ: Prentice Hall Regents.

Knight, G. H. (1985). The Geometry of Maori Art – Weaving Patterns. In *NZ Mathematics Magazine,* 21(3) 80–87.

Kyselka, W. (1987). *An Ocean in Mind.* Honolulu: University of Hawai'i Press.

Lakatos, I. (1976). *Proofs and Refutations.* Cambridge: Cambridge University Press.

Lakatos, I. (1978). *Mathematics, Science and Epistemology. Philosophical Papers Vol. 2.,* J. Worrall & G. Currie (Eds), Cambridge: Cambridge University Press.

Lakoff, G. (1987). *Women, Fire and Dangerous Things: What Categories Reveal About the Mind.* Chicago: Chicago University Press.

Lakoff, G. & Johnson, M. (1980). *Metaphors We Live By.* Chicago: University of Chicago Press.

Lakoff, G. & Johnson, M. (1999). *Philosophy in the Flesh: The Embodied Mind and Its Challenge to Western Thought.* New York: Basic Books.

Lakoff, G. & Núñez, R. E. (2000). *Where Mathematics Comes From: How the Embodied Mind Brings Mathematics into Being.* New York: Basic Books.

Lasserre, F. (1964). *The Birth of Mathematics in the Age of Plato.* Trans. H. Mortimer. London: Hutchinson.

Lean, G. A. (1995). Unpublished PhD Thesis, Papua New Guinea University of Technology, Lae, Papua New Guinea.

Lee, P. (1996). *The Whorf Theory Complex: A Critical Reconstruction.* Amsterdam: John Benjamins Publishing Company.

Lewis, D. (1975). *We, the Navigators: The Ancient Art of Landfinding in the Pacific.* Canberra: Australian National University Press.

Lipke, J., Yanez, E., & Andrew–Ihrke, D. (2006). A Two–Way Process for Developing Culturally–Based Math: Examples from Math in a Cultural Context. Presented to the 3rd International Conference on Ethnomathematics, Auckland. Available at http://www.math.auckland.ac.nz.

Lizcano, E. (1993). *Imaginario colectivo y creación matemática. La construcción social de número, el espacio y lo imposible en China y en Grecia.* Barcelona: Gedisa.

McConaghy, C. (2000). *Rethinking Indigenous Education: Culturalism, Colonialism and the Poltiics of Knowing.* Flaxton, Queensland, Australia: Post Pressed.

Mac Lane, S. (1981). Mathematical Models: A sketch for the philosophy of mathematics. *American Mathematical Monthly, 88*(7).

Mac Lane, S. (1998). *Categories for the Working Mathematician (2nd ed.). Graduate Texts in Mathematics 5.* Springer.

Madden, J. J. (2001). Book Review: Where Mathematics Comes From. *Notices of the American Mathematical Society, 48*(10), 1182–1188.

Menninger, K. (1969). *Number Words and Number Symbols: A Cultural History of Numbers.* (Translated by Paul Broneer). Cambridge, MA: The MIT Press.

Metge, J. (1978). *Talking Past Each Other: Problems of Cross–Cultural Communication.* Wellington: Victoria University Press.

Meyer, D. L. & Collier, R. O. (Eds.) (1970). *Bayesian Statistics: Ninth Annual Phi Delta Kappa Symposium on Educational Research.* Bloomington, Indiana: F. E. Peacock Publishers Inc.

Miura, I. T., Okamoto, Y., Kim, C. C., Chang, C–M., Steere, M., & Fayol, M. (1994). Comparisons of children's cognitive representation of number: China, France, Japan, Korea, Sweden, and the United States. *International Journal of Behavioral Development, 77*, 401–411.

Monteiro, M. de (Ed.) (2002). *Proceedings of the Second International Congress on Ethnomathematics (ICEM2),* CD Rom, Lyrium Comunacacao Ltda, Ouro Preto, Brazil.

Moore, J. (1997). *Visions of Culture: An Introduction to Anthropological Theories and Theorists.* Walnut Creek, CA: AltaMitra Press.

Moschkovich, J. N. (2002). A situated and sociocultural perspective on bilingual mathematics learners. *Mathematical Thinking and Learning, Special issue on Equity,* N. Nassir and P. Cobb, editors *4*(2&3), 189–212.

Nathan, G., Trinick, T., Tobin, E., & Barton, B. (1993). Tahi Rua, Toru, Wha; Mathematics Counts in Māori Renaissance. In M. Stephens, A. Wayward, D. Clark & J. Izard (Eds.) *Communicating Mathematics: Perspectives from Classroom Practise and Current Research,* p. 291–300, Melbourne: Australian Council for Educational Research Ltd.

Neville–Barton, P. & Barton, B. (2004). *The Relationship Between English Language and Mathematics Learning for Non–Native Speakers: A TLRI Research Report for NZCER,* Wellington: New Zealand Council for Education Research.

New Zealand Ministry of Education. (1991). *Nga Kupu Tikanga Pangarau.* Wellington: Learning Media.

New Zealand Ministry of Education. (1994). *Pangarau: Te Tauaki Marautanga,* Wellington: Learning Media.

New Zealand Ministry of Education. (1995). *Te Papakupu Pangarau,* Wellington: Learning Media.

Ohia, M. (1993). Adapting Mathematics to Meet Maori Needs and Aspirations: An Attempt to Shift Paradigms, *SAMEpapers 93*, p. 104–15.

Owens, K. (2001). The Work of Glendon Lean on the Counting Systems of Papua New Guinea and Oceania. *Mathematics Education Research Journal, 13*(1), 47–71.

Papert, S. (1980). *Mindstorms: Children, Computers, and Powerful Ideas*. New York: Basic Books.

Pendergrast, M. (1984). Maori Plaiting Patterns: Raranga Whakairo. Coromandel, NZ: Coromandel Press.

Pendergrast, M. (1987). Te Aho Tapu. The Sacred Thread. Traditional Maori Weaving. Auckland, NZ: Reed Methuen.

Piaget, J. (1953). *The Origin of Intelligence in the Child*. Translated M. Cook). London: Routledge & Paul.

Pinker, S. (1994). *The Language Instinct: How The Mind Creates Language*. New York: HarperCollins Inc.

Pinxten, R., van Dooren, I., & Harvey, F. (1983). *The Anthropology of Space: Explorations into the Natural Philosophy and Semantics of the Navajo*. Philadelphia: University of Philadelphia Press.

Pinxten, R., van Dooren, I. & Soberon, E. (1987). *Towards a Navajo Indian Geometry*. Gent: K.K.I. Books.

Powell, A. & Frankenstein, M. (1997). *Ethnomathematics: Challenging Eurocentrism in Mathematics Education*. Albany: State University of New York Press, 1997.

Restivo, S. (1983). *The Social Relations of Physics, Mysticism, and Mathematics*. Dordrecht: D. Reidel.

Restivo, S. (1992). *Mathematics in Society and History: Sociological Enquiries*. Dordrecht: Kluwer Academic Publishers.

Restivo, S. (1993). The Social Life of Mathematics. In S. Restivo, J. P. Van Bendegem & R. Fischer (Eds) *Math Worlds: Philosophical and Social Studies of Mathematics and Mathematics Education*, New York: State University of New York Press.

Restivo, S., Van Bendegem, J. P. & Fischer, R. (Eds.) (1993). *Math Worlds: Philosophical and Social Studies of Mathematics and Mathematics Education*. Albany, NY: State University of New York Press.

Robinson, A. (1966). *Non–Standard Analysis*. Amsterdam: North–Holland.

Rotman, B. (1987). *Signifying Nothing: The Semiotics of Zero*. Stanford, CA: Stanford University Press.

Russell, B. (1946). *History of Western Philosophy*. London: George Allen and Unwin.

Sacks, O. (1991). *Seeing Voices: A Journey into the world of the Deaf*. London: Picador.

Senft, G. (1997). *Referring to Space: Studies in Austronesian and Papuan Languages*. Oxford: Clarendon Press.

Setati, M. & Adler, J. (2001). Between Languages and Discourses: Language Practices in Primary Multilingual Mathematics Classrooms in South Africa, *Educational Studies in Mathematics, 43*(3), 243–269.

Shanker, S. (1987). *Wittgenstein and the Turning–Point in the Philosophy of Mathematics*. London: Croom Helm Ltd.

Singmaster, D. (2006). *Chronology of Recreational Mathematics*. <http://www.eldar.org/~problemi/singmast/recchron.html> (Accessed May, 2006).

Siromoney, R. (1986). Array Languages and Lindenmayer Systems. In G. Rosenberg & A. Saomaa (Eds.), *The Book of L*, p. 413–426. Heidelberg: Springer–Verlag.

Siromnoey, G. & Siromoney, R. (1987). Rosefeld's cycle grammars and kolam. In H. Ehry, M. Nagl, A. Rosenfeld, & G. Rosenberg (Eds.), *Graph–Grammars and their Application to Computer Science. Third International Workshop, 1986. Lecture Notes in Computer Science, No. 291,* p. 565–579, Berlin: Springer–Verlag.

Smith, R. C. (1982). *Gaston Bachelard*. Boston: Twayne Publishers.

Sobel, D. (1995). *Longitude: The True Story of a Lone Genius who solved the Greatest Scientific Problem of his Time*. New York: Walker & Co.

Spengler, O. (1926). *The Decline of the West: Form and Actuality*. C. F. Atkinson (trans.). London: Knopf.

Spengler, O. (1956). Meaning of Numbers. In *The World of Mathematics, Vol IV*, p. 2315–2347, London: George Allen & Unwin Ltd.

Strauss, C. (2000). The Culture Concept and the Individualism–Collectivism Debate: Dominant and Alternative Attributions for Class in the United States. In L. Nucci, G. Saxe & E. Turiel (Eds.), *Culture, Thought, and Development*. NJ:Lawrence Earlbaum Associates, Inc.

Stigler, J. & Baranes, R. (1988). Culture and Mathematics Learning. In E. Z. Rothkopf (ed) *Review of Research in Education*, 15, 253–305. Washington, DC: American Educational Research Association.

Stillwell, J. (1989). *Mathematics and Its History*. New York: Springer.

Swetz, F. (1974). *Mathematics Education in China: Its Growth and Development*. Cambridge, MA: MIT Press.

Swetz, F. (1987). *Capitalism and Arithmetic: The New Math of the 15th Century*. La Salle, Illinois: Open Court.

Swetz, F. & Kao, T. (1977). *Was Pythagoras Chinese? An Examination of Right Triangle Theory in Ancient China*. University Park: Pennsylvania State University Press.

Tambiah, S. (1990). *Magic, Science, Religion, and the Scope of Rationality*. Cambridge: Cambridge University Press.

Tiles, M. (1984). *Bachelard: Science and Objectivity*. Cambridge: Cambridge University Press.

Tobias, S. (1995). *Overcoming Math Anxiety*. New York: W. W. Norton & Co.

Thom, R. (1992). Leaving Mathematics for Philosophy. In C. Casacuberta & Castellet, M. (Eds) *Mathematical Research Today and Tomorrow: Viewpoints of Seven Fields Medalists. Lecture Notes in Mathematics 1525*, p. 1–12, Berlin: Springer–Verlag.

Thomas, S. (1987). *The Last Navigator*. New York: Random House.

Trinick, T. (1999). *The Relationships between Maori Culture and Maori Mathematical Language*. Unpublished Masters thesis, The University of Auckland.

Turnbull, D. (1991). *Mapping the World in Mind: An Investigation of the Unwritten Knowledge of the Micronesian Navigators*, Geelong: Deakin University Press.

Waite, J. (1990). Another Look at the Actor Emphatic, *Journal of the Polynesian Society, 99*, 395–413.

Welsch, W. (1999) 'Transculturality: The Puzzling Form of Cultures Today'. In M. Featherstone & S. Lash (Eds.), *Spaces of Cultures: City – Nation – World,* London: Sage Publications Ltd.

Weyl, I. H. (1944). Obituary: David Hilbert 1862–1943. RSBIOS, 4, 547–553.

Wigner, E. (1960). The Unreasonable Effectiveness of Mathematics in the Natural Sciences. *Communications in Pure and Applied Mathematics*, 13(1).

Witherspoon, G. (1977). *Language and Art in the Navajo Universe*. Ann Arbor: University of Michigan Press.

Wittgenstein, L. (1956). *Remarks on the Foundations of Mathematics*. Oxford: Blackwell.

Whorf, B. (1956) Languages and Logic. In J. Carroll (Ed.) *Language, Thought and Reality: Selected Writings by Benjamin Lee Whorf*, Cambridge, MA, MIT Press.

Index to Names

Index to Subjects

Mathematics Education Library

Managing Editor: A.J. Bishop, Melbourne, Australia

H. Steinbring: The Construction of New Mathematical Knowledge in Classroom Interaction: An Epistemological Perspective. 2005. ISBN 0-387-24251-1

M.Borba, M. Villarreal: Humans-with-Media and the Reorganization of Mathematical Thinking: Information and Communication Technologies, Modeling, Visualization and Experimentation. 2005. ISBN 0-387-24263-5 HB; ISBN 0-387-32821-1 PB

G. Jones (ed): Exploring Probability in School: Challenges for Teaching and Learning. 2005. ISBN 0-387-24529-4

D. DeBock, W. Van Dooren, D. Janssens, and L. Verschaffel: The Illusion of Linearity: From Analysis to Improvement. 2007. ISBN 978-0-387-71082-2

K. Francois and J. P. Van Bendegem: Philosophical Dimensions in Mathematics Education. 2007. ISBN 978-0-387-71571-1

E. Filloy, L. Puig, and T. Rojano: Educational Algebra: A Theoretical and Empirical Approach. 2007. ISBN 978-0-387-71253-6

B. Barton: The Language of Mathematics. 2007. ISBN 978-0-387-72858-2

P. Winbourne, A. Watson: New Directions for Situated Cognition in Mathematics Education. 2007. ISBN 978-0-387-71577-3

E. DeFreitas, K. Nolan: Opening the Research Text. 2007. ISBN 978-0-387-75463-5

Printed in the United States
105121LV00001B/11/A